T0129910

JIM GARDNER

BALBOA.PRESS
A DIVISION OF HAY HOUSE

Balboa Press books may be ordered through booksellers or by contacting:

Balboa Press
A Division of Hay House
1663 Liberty Drive
Bloomington, IN 47403
www.balboapress.com
1 (877) 407-4847

Because of the dynamic nature of the Internet, any web addresses or links contained in this book may have changed since publication and may no longer be valid. The views expressed in this work are solely those of the author and do not necessarily reflect the views of the publisher, and the publisher hereby disclaims any responsibility for them.

The author of this book does not dispense medical advice or prescribe the use of any technique as a form of treatment for physical, emotional, or medical problems without the advice of a physician, either directly or indirectly. The intent of the author is only to offer information of a general nature to help you in your quest for emotional and spiritual well-being. In the event you use any of the information in this book for yourself, which is your constitutional right, the author and the publisher assume no responsibility for your actions.

Any people depicted in stock imagery provided by Getty Images are models, and such images are being used for illustrative purposes only. Certain stock imagery © Getty Images.

Print information available on the last page.

ISBN: 978-1-9822-4886-4 (sc)
ISBN: 978-1-9822-4888-8 (hc)
ISBN: 978-1-9822-4887-1 (e)

Library of Congress Control Number: 2020910246

Balboa Press rev. date: 06/16/2020

Contents

Introduction vii

Chapter 1   Having the Heart for the Art 1
Chapter 2   What Is the Purpose of Art? 15
Chapter 3   Creating the Masterpiece 31
Chapter 4   The Keys to Happiness and the Keys to
            Success 43
Chapter 5   Talent and Curiosity......................................53
Chapter 6   Courage and Confidence 59
Chapter 7   The Creative Power of Thoughts and Beliefs 71
Chapter 8   The Art of Creating the Life We Want............83
Chapter 9   There Is No Competition to Being Yourself.....93

The Summary 97
About the Author 101

Introduction

Why am I writing this book?

My intention in writing this book is to encourage you to make the most of your unique gifts and talents so you can live a creatively productive life that provides a benefit to the community you live in while being a source of prosperity, fulfillment, and satisfaction for yourself.

I will encourage you to follow your heart and to listen to that still, small voice within, as you develop your intuition and see where it takes you. My hope is that you will pursue your personal interests in such a way that you can earn a living by applying what you learn, and blend it with your unique talents to serve the needs of the community you live in.

I have lived a very enjoyable life, first as an entertainer (which ruined me for any kind of a normal day job), and now as an artist. I'm not saying I've lived an easy life, but I am saying I've lived a very fun-filled and enjoyable life. I believe I have lived the life I was *meant* to live. I've had my dark times and my challenging times, when I felt I wasn't up to the task and I wanted to quit. Those moments turned out to be opportunities to reflect and a time to assess and readjust my direction. Those moments were significant times of growth, as they marked the end of one era and the beginning of the next.

I learned the keys to happiness and the keys to success at an early age, and I'll share them with you here.

The key to happiness is to figure out what you like to do and then find a way to get paid to do it.

The key to success is that you can do anything you like to do, as long as you do it in a way that benefits others.

People don't pay us for the work we do; they pay us for the *benefit they receive* from the work we do. A financially successful life as a creative person is all about using our talents to benefit others in some way. That also happens to be the key to running a successful business of any kind. A business exists to do for others what they can't do for themselves. The business of art is no different.

Life has so much to offer, and there is so much to do that there is no reason for any person with talent not to be busy and productive. The key is to be busy in such a way that you can earn a good income with your activities.

For the creative person, these are very exciting times. Creative opportunities are everywhere. With the internet, your opportunities to market your creative ideas and products to the entire world have been placed in your hands—literally!

We all absorb things from the world around us, and we all contribute back to society in one way or another. Each of us contributes something to our community when we show up for work, when we purchase things at the store, and when we consciously or unconsciously participate in the social culture of our generation.

When we think of ourselves as professional artists, we are making a conscious decision that we want to contribute to the world by using our talents in some creative way, and *we want to be compensated* for our contribution. Our art is more than a hobby; it's a business, and it needs to earn a profit.

As artists, we absorb ideas from the world around us, and we make use of the many tools and materials available to us. Then we express ourselves in some way that gives something back to society as our personal interpretation of how we feel, and we call it *art*. We write songs, novels, and poems. We paint symbols, words, and pictures. We create jewelry and decorative items that enhance our sense of beauty and our surroundings.

The way we express ourselves can take many forms. Some of us express ourselves with tangible works of art, while others of us express our creative urges through various forms of service, such as interior decorators, entertainers, and musical performers, poets and dancers.

This is a fantastic time to be a creatively minded person. I'm writing this book for you to use in developing a creative lifestyle that is financially rewarding as well as emotionally satisfying and spiritually fulfilling.

You may not always have a job, but you always have a purpose. If you know what your purpose is, then your job is to fulfill your purpose.

Please enjoy your unique talents and share them with others. The world is waiting for your gifts, and only you can give them.

Jim Gardner
May 2020

Chapter 1

HAVING THE HEART FOR THE ART

Attitude is everything.

In my first book, *Artists Are Like Apple Trees,* I made the point that apple trees produce apples, but they have no use for their own product. However, if they stop producing apples, the tree soon dies, because there is no reason for the nourishment from the soil to travel throughout the tree if there is no fruit to nourish at the end of the branches.

Creative people are the same way. We must use it or we will lose it. While we may continue to walk and talk and stand upright, that creative part of us will die—or at least go into deep hiding if it's not acknowledged and put to use. For those of us who actually want to earn a living with our talents, we must find ways to make use of our creative abilities in such a way that people will be willing to pay us.

That leads us to the question of *how do we earn money?* The most basic answer to that question is: we only earn money by providing some form of service or by providing some type of product that serves a purpose in someone else's life. That product or service must be valued enough by others that they are willing to pay for it. How much they are willing to pay

1

would be determined by how much they value it. As creative and expressive people, there are no limits to the many ways we can serve the needs of others while we satisfy our own financial and emotional needs.

In this book, I use the term *artist* in a way that applies to any form of personal self-expression. Regardless of how we choose to express ourselves, the rules for earning money remain the same: people pay for services and products that benefit them!

Understanding that statement will lead us to the question of what *kind* of service do *I* want to provide? How do *I* enjoy expressing myself? Do I think in terms of creating decorative artwork to hang on the wall, or do I prefer to make jewelry or tattoos to decorate the body? Do I enjoy expressing myself with digital or three-dimensional art, or do I prefer to express myself through entertainment and the production of music, drama, poetry, or dance? It's these kinds of questions that we must ask ourselves in order to establish a base of operation for us to begin.

This book is all about you. And it's about designing and living the kind of life *you* want to live. Your life can be as creative as any work of art, made up of many interrelated parts strung together on a day-to-day basis, composed of all the love, passion, hopes, and challenges of any heroic epic. It will be a continuous work in progress.

Once we decide what kind of life we want to live, we can assess what we have to work with in regard to our talents, our interests, our available materials and tools, and where we might find the market for our art. With today's internet, the market for many forms of creative expression has blossomed. Anything with interesting visual impact or emotional attraction can be shared around the world at minimal cost. The traditional forms of marketing can still work in the form of person-to-person art shows, local art galleries, and developing a personal client base. It's usually best to bloom where you're planted, to make the most of what's in front of you.

Once we've established who we want to become, then we can set a direction for ourselves to go in and define our market. The real goal of everything we do is to live the kind of life *we* want to live. And to do that, we must find ways to satisfy the needs of others through the effective use of what we are offering.

It's possible to earn a living from any form of self-expression, *as long as it benefits someone in some way.* People pay for benefits. The rules of art, such as color and balance, rhythm and form, music and pictures, to name a few, apply to many seemingly unrelated industries and occupations. But there is a thread of similarity flowing through it all. For example, learning about the effects of stage lighting and set design applies to theater and movie production, as well as designing storefront windows and sales displays for trade shows and business conventions. The same rules of using color and balance, rhythm and contrast apply to all sorts of creative expression, and each form can be turned into a profitable type of creative service. *People pay for the benefit they believe they will get from something,* and that is the key to earning a living in any line of work!

It all starts with attitude.

Our attitude about things determines how we treat those things. That includes our attitude about ourselves, how we feel about our sense of purpose, and our definition of success.

Success is a personal thing, and it requires a personal definition. Success is not something that someone else wants for us, but rather, it is our own definition of fulfillment and satisfaction that matters. That includes our sense of self-esteem and our definition of reward.

What is "it" that drives us and fires up our passion? What do we desire most from our lives? Fame? Fortune? Liberty? Adventure? A deepening sense of self-discovery? A deeper sense of purpose?

The list can go on and on, and it will be different for everyone. If there were a common thread, I believe it would be a desire for a sense of fulfillment, a feeling that what we do does matter, and that our time on earth means something to someone other than ourselves. *We want to leave our mark!*

Some of us want to leave our mark, *and* we want to get paid to do it. If we want to get paid consistently for doing something we love, it requires us to view that passion as a business or to think of it as a career. It requires long-term planning and goals, and it results in building a reputation over time. It also requires that we be professional about how we express ourselves.

We have to see our unique creative abilities as being our gifts that have been given to us to share with the world. We must see our unique gifts as a way to feed ourselves and as a way for us to get the things we want in life that only money can buy. It means we must be willing to exchange our time and our talents for dollars. It means we are in the business of producing an art form with the intention of selling it in exchange for money. It means we want to elevate the quality of our self-expression to the point where it has value to other people such that they are willing and eager to pay for it.

The business of art is no different than any other business.

The only reason any kind of business exists is for the simple reason of providing a product or service to others that they cannot provide for themselves. The mechanic repairs my car because I don't have the proper tools or the necessary skills. The real estate agent helps me locate a home and processes the paperwork because I don't have the experience, knowledge, or skills to do everything that's needed. The performing artist provides entertainment with their dance or musical expression, and the visual artist provides a product or service that in some way serves the design or decorative needs of the marketplace.

When people value something, they are willing to pay for it. We just have to let them know that it's available, and today there are many ways to do that. We'll discuss some of those ways throughout this book.

When we exchange our time and talents for money, we are engaging in commerce. As artists, we seek commissions for our work. That's how we survive! Artists need customers, just like any other business, and we *want* people to hire us to do the kind of work we offer. However, many creative people want to avoid being labeled as commercial artists, yet we all would like to get paid for using our talents. This is an internal conflict between our head and our heart as we struggle with our definitions and our conscience, between wanting to be pure and true to our art and wanting to be appreciated by those who are willing to pay for it.

This attitude about being negatively labeled for selling out to commercialism is related to the thought that we are selling out our soul just to make a buck. But if the alternative is to work in a job that doesn't require any of our unique talents, then we are already selling out our creative spirit just to make a buck by doing something for money that is not very satisfying or spiritually fulfilling. We must respect and honor that creative part of us by putting it to good use and making this world better for someone while we benefit ourselves.

If our heart is in the art, and we are willing to serve the needs of others, then in the bigger picture, the work we are producing is helping to make someone else's life better. So I say *do it!* We are all here to serve others in some way. The world does not owe us a living, but we owe it to ourselves to be all that we can be. We already have the potential within us, and all we have to do is develop our gifts into a product or service that serves the needs of others. Our success is really a matter of attitude.

Like the apple tree, we may have no personal use for the products we produce, but we need to continually participate in the process of producing something, or the ability to imagine and produce things will die within us. If the imagination isn't nourished with encouragement, the creative urge that is so strong in every child becomes buried or hidden behind the everyday practical concerns of living. As human beings, we all come here with lessons to learn, and we've each been given unique strengths or gifts to work with. If we use our gifts, we will learn our lessons, and life will be filled with adventures and meaningful experiences that only those who go on the journey of self-discovery and creative expression will know. If we don't use our gifts, we may find employment and earn a good income, but we will never know the sense of fulfillment and feel the confidence that comes from being the whole, unique person we have the potential to be. Our ultimate masterpiece of a life well lived will require balancing our physical health with our emotional self-expression, along with using our intellectual ability to earn money by doing meaningful work that fulfills our individual purpose for being here.

If your form of expression makes the world a better place in some way, then you owe it to the world to put it where it can do the most good. It may be helpful to realize that some of the greatest artists known to us today, such as Michelangelo and Leonardo da Vinci started their careers in commercial art production shops, where they developed their techniques through on-the-job training. They worked as production artists alongside other artists, while the master artist and shop owner guided their training and added the finishing touches.

Once they mastered their skills, they left the shops, went out on their own, and sought commissions from wealthy patrons of their day, such as the Medici family and the popes and emperors. They were commissioned to produce the works of art that have made them famous. They were commercial artists in the truest sense of the word. They participated in "production shops," where the master sketched the basics, the assistants filled in some of the parts, and the master came back in and added the refinements. Collaborations of that sort were the normal way of producing art in those days. There was a market for art (especially religious themes) and there were artists who were ready and able to fill that need. They often hired assistants to help them when they were needed, and they had student apprentices who would copy the master's work with the intention of selling the copies, since copying devices such as we have today did not exist. Many legitimate copies of their works still exist today as a result of the commercial practices of that time.

The great masters started their careers in production shops and developed their skills on the job as they built their reputations in and around their communities. They worked with other artists in the production shops, and they learned from each other as they collaborated on large projects with popular and common themes of their day. When artists completed their apprenticeship, they left the studios and went out on their own. They competed in the marketplace for commissions, and they hired assistants to help them when they were needed.

Artwork was their business, and the famous artists didn't always work alone or in isolation. Rather, they were part of an industry that was an integral part of their society. Because the power of the image has always been used as a way to communicate an idea to the public, wealthy patrons would commission artists to portray them in favorable and praising fashion, much like advertising does today. Some things never change.

If you feel you're caught in the kind of situation where you want to be free to do your own thing and you want to avoid being too commercial, but you still want to earn a good living with your talents, then let's take a look at that dilemma. In order to do that, we have to take a look at ourselves. We need to establish some priorities and determine what is important to us as individuals. Designing our own life is in itself a creative process, and our entire life becomes our ultimate work of art.

It's *your* life that you're expressing, and it's *your* life that you're experiencing at any moment. Again, *being successful depends on your personal definition* of what success is and not necessarily on the definition of success that's shown in commercials for get-rich-quick schemes and ads that promote every little thing that glitters.

Success requires blending and balancing a number of things. It requires imagination and creativity, a vision or definition of what we want to achieve and what we want to be successful at. There needs to be an adequate financial reward mixed with an inner feeling of satisfaction that comes from taking pride in our work. We also need a healthy body and a healthy mental outlook on life, mixed with some social interaction and so forth.

Essentially, there are four areas that need to be in balance in order for us to feel whole and complete as human beings: our physical health, our emotional ability to express ourselves, our intellectual ability to solve problems, and a feeling that our lives are meaningful on some level. I will address each of these areas in more detail as we develop our concept of art and we learn how to express ourselves more effectively in each area.

Having the heart for the art operates on several levels. It starts with the urge to express ourselves beyond just words and conversation. We *want* to learn to play an instrument or paint a picture. We love to sing or dance, and we wish we could do it all better. Perhaps we love the glitter and the glamour, and we want to be rich and famous as a movie star or rock star. Whatever it is that excites us, *it all starts with a desire* to be a certain type of person or to have a certain kind of result. *Desire is the starting point for all accomplishment.*

Having a clear vision of what we want triggers our imagination to find ways to accomplish the things we desire. Once we've imagined the end result we're going after, it's important to believe it's possible to achieve that result. There's never a guarantee that everything will work out, but that's the adventure of it all! Often it's the adventure of going on the journey that is more motivating for the creative person than actually accomplishing the end result. It's more fun to do things just to prove to ourselves that we can do them. Another way of saying it is that it's the journey, not the destination that makes the trip worthwhile.

To succeed, we need to take on the mentality of the Olympic athlete. There is no guarantee that we will make it into the Olympics, but just the challenge of developing ourselves to the point of being good enough to try is exciting. Wanting something that's bigger than our current situation brings out the best in anyone who goes on that journey.

Without wanting to produce Olympic quality in our work, it's unlikely that it will happen by itself. We must have the desire to be the best we can be and to give our best at whatever form of expression we take.

Today we're living with a false sense of security if we think our current job or occupation will last forever. As technology takes over many jobs, and companies are bought and sold to other conglomerates around the world, our definition of job security has to change. It must come from our own willingness to serve others. Flexibility and creativity go hand in hand. Success depends on being able to create solutions for the situations of this moment.

You may not always have a job, but you always have a purpose. If you know what your purpose is, then your job is to fulfill your purpose.

A life that is lived with a sense of purpose requires you to be on a mission of sorts. Your job becomes more than just a paycheck. It becomes a way for you to make a difference and leave your mark.

Having a sense of purpose for our lives raises the value of what we do to a level beyond simply earning money. Having a sense of purpose in life means that we direct all our daily activities toward the greater effect we want to have on our community and on the planet as a whole.

There is no security in this world, but that shouldn't frighten us. I know it sounds harsh, but once we accept that there are no guarantees about anything, then we can stop looking for it or wishing things were different. We can get on with the joy of creating what we're here to create *now* as we do our part toward making this world better in some way.

You've probably heard the statement, "Where there's a will, there's a way." Having the heart for the art requires us to be willing to take on the challenges of personal growth and continued self-improvement. Our ability to express ourselves is a direct result of our current state of mind or our current level of development. We can only express what we are, and we can only give what we have. If we want to offer more, we must develop it within ourselves first.

Will power, commitment, and dedication all play a part in determining our level of success in any endeavor. Each of us must first have the desire for something, and then we must have the courage to take the first few steps and get started, and then we need the commitment to follow through and finish what we started.

If we have the desire and willingness to take ourselves on as creative and expressive people, then we have the foundation for a great and adventurous career that will be as exciting and satisfying for us as it is beneficial to the community we serve.

It's important to understand that no one is born with talent. We are born with a natural curiosity that urges us to explore our surroundings by crawling around corners and climbing up stairs and so forth. It's only when our curiosity is encouraged in some way, such as developing the skills of catching a moving ball or learning to color inside the lines that we actually develop our curiosity into a skill.

Once a skill reaches a level of development that goes beyond what is considered to be average, other people see our skills as talents, and *they* give us the label of being talented. However, talents are developed. They're not just given to some and denied to others. Talents are really nothing more than skills that have been developed to a level of excellence; skills are simply things that were developed in response to our personal interests and the encouragements we received along the way.

If we feel that we are not talented enough to succeed at something, then it's really just a matter of developing a greater interest in the subject and applying some practice with the tools or instruments that are required.

Investing in our talents is the smartest investment we can make! The more we use our talents, the greater they become. *Talents expand and improve with use.* Physical objects don't do that. Physical objects wear out the more we use them. Talents and skills improve and expand the more we use them. We must invest in ourselves. We are worth it, and our talents are our greatest assets.

When starting out in any career, it's helpful to remember that it's not how much we earn but how much we learn that's important. Every job we take on should be seen as an opportunity to learn something new that will help us be the person we want to be. The creative lifestyle becomes a lifelong learning process that honors our curiosity about new things while it satisfies our need to contribute to our community, as we continually discover new ways to get paid in return for the services we provide.

When we're young and just beginning our career, it's

important to work with other people that we can learn from. I suggest seeing each job we apply for as being a paid educational opportunity and not as an end result in itself. We may not want to say that on our job application form, but in reality, we want to keep learning new things. When we stop learning new things, we stop being creative. We fall into patterns of repetition, and the excitement of learning comes to a halt. Who wants to get stuck in a boring, repetitive, nine-to-five job or lifestyle? That lifestyle may offer a sense of job security, but repetition kills creativity. By definition, repetition means doing the same thing over and over again, while being creative means doing something that hasn't been done before. It's a lot more fun to be creative!

Chapter 2

WHAT IS THE PURPOSE OF ART?

As a professional artist, it's helpful to understand the bigger purpose that art serves in our lives, from both the personal perspective of the artist, as well as from the historical perspective of how art has influenced societies throughout time. That requires understanding the effect art has on us personally, as well as the effect our art has on the people who experience it.

As artists, we absorb a multitude of influences from all around us, and we process those experiences through our emotions and imaginations. Then we express ourselves in a way that gives something back to the community, and we call it art.

From the earliest known cave paintings to the latest high-tech videos, artwork has been used to affect the public in some way. The visual image leaves its mark on the minds and memories of those who experience it. There is *power* in the visual image, and as professional artists, we have the opportunity to control and manipulate the image such that it has the effect on the public that we want it to have.

One effect we want our artwork to have on people is that we want them to buy it. That means we have to influence them emotionally with the feeling of desire. They have to want what we are offering before they will be willing to pay for it. So, what does our ideal market want? For that answer, we must define our ideal market, and it will be different for each of us.

Let's start with you. What do you desire? What kind of lifestyle do you want? Once you know what kind of a life you want to create for yourself, you can figure out what path you might take to get that result. Are you looking for consistent employment in the form of a steady job, or do you prefer the independence of being self-employed, working for a variety of clients rather than one steady employer?

Each approach to earning an income has its benefits and its drawbacks. You may prefer to market your personal services to other businesses such as advertising agencies, sign shops, and screen printers. Some of these businesses hire artists for steady work in their own art departments. As an employee, you can get all the benefits the company offers, but also all the frustrations of corporate life, such as punching a clock, supervisors looking over your shoulder, and so forth. Some corporate work can remain fresh and exciting, while often, steady work turns into repetitive production work and lacks the joy of learning new things.

Another option is to be a private vendor or freelancer who works with individual businesses as their outside independent artist. This gives you the ability to set your own prices and work your own schedule, work from your own studio, and be responsible for your own bookkeeping and running the business. The benefit for your client is that their business is not responsible for your ongoing costs such as insurance, vacation pay, and so forth, and your expense is a simple write-off for their accounting department.

Perhaps the biggest question to consider is the type of

artwork you enjoy doing. The real goal of this book is to help you live an enjoyable life by applying the gifts you've been given in ways that serve the needs of the world. But it all starts with you and deciding how you want to satisfy yourself. This whole book is about you and your life and what you want to do with it. *The first work of art you want to create is yourself.*

To create a masterpiece, the artist must be a master. You can't give away something you don't have, so let's start by asking ourselves: What do *I* have to offer? What do I enjoy doing the most? Do I like to work with my hands, perhaps forming pottery out of clay or gluing pieces of unrelated stuff into fascinating sculptures? Do I prefer pixels over pigments? Do I enjoy spreading paint with a brush or spraying it and sponging it onto things? Am I fascinated by three-dimensional objects or abstract shapes with colors and textures? Do I enjoy combining sounds with movement to create dances and then add backdrops of colored lights, graphics, and unexpected objects? Wow! It's all art, and it all impacts us when we create it or when we experience it. The real starting point and most important question for each of us to ask is where do I find my joy? Once we can answer that, the trick is to combine the various things that bring us pleasure into a product or service that can benefit someone else in some way.

The things that bring us pleasure are the things we should be sharing with the world.

Passion is the raw material we use to express ourselves. When our passions rage with anger, it shows. When we are filled with passionate love for something, that shows as well. There's really no hiding how we feel, and we are expressing our feelings in everything we do. As artists, we express our feelings visually. As singers, we express our feelings with our voices. As playwrights and authors, we express our passions with drama and words. We all have our own way of expressing ourselves, and if we channel our feelings into the appropriate forms, we can actually get paid for expressing how we feel.

When we express our joyful emotions, the products and services we create are filled with the passion we are feeling when we create those things. Our emotional state of mind affects the results of anything we do. I think this is especially evident in contemporary music, where performing artists can express themselves with sentimental love songs sung from the heart or screaming violent rock lyrics combined with explosive concert performances. It's all art, and it's all self-expression, and there's a market for all of it. We each get to choose what we want to contribute and what form we want our contribution to take.

Some artists prefer to specialize in doing a specific type of illustration, such as small images for children's books, tattoos, greeting cards, or T-shirt designs. These types of visual arts involve a small image that impacts the eye and makes an immediate impression on the mind of the viewer. Greeting cards and T-shirt designs offer your customers an opportunity to express their feelings by using your thoughts and words in ways that they aren't able to do for themselves.

Regardless of how we choose to express ourselves, we will attract the attention of people who relate to our style or message, because we are giving them a way to express themselves through our products. People are willing to pay for that kind of product or service because we have a way of saying it so much better than they can.

Earning significant amounts of money with the artwork

that is used on T-shirts and greeting cards requires the added steps of printing the image and establishing a distribution process. The internet and today's print-on-demand technologies have made both steps simpler and less expensive than ever before. You can earn a small profit by selling your designs or the rights to the original artwork to your client, and you'll get paid one time for creating the design. That is the situation you're in when you are a staff artist and you get the paycheck, but the rights to the design belong to the company. You can earn larger profits by keeping the rights to the original artwork and collecting a royalty or a percentage of the sale price for each item that's sold with your design on it. This involves some legal contracts and paperwork to track sales.

Huge profits for artwork can be made when you sell the same design over and over again by applying it to several different items such as posters, shirts, collectable plates, and similar gift items. Think of the T-shirt and souvenir sales at sporting events and rock concerts. There's a lot of profit in that industry. Often sports figures and celebrities make more profit from souvenir sales than they do on their performances, but the items they sell start with an interesting graphic element, and that's where the artist comes in. Without the image, it's nothing special.

Coming up with new artwork and designs can keep any artist busy by creating items that have a seasonal or short-term value, such as promotional art that is used to celebrate a specific event with a location, time, and date. Designs used for greeting cards are seasonal or meant for special occasions, and they need to be constantly recreated, thereby becoming a form of steady work for the creative illustrator. Blend your sense of humor with your drawing skills or combine your beautiful illustrations with the kindness of your poetry, and you have the making of a very profitable business.

There is always a need for new artwork that can be printed onto T-shirts for special events and trending social situations. Wearable art with a strong graphic statement can be used as a visually effective way for people to express their feelings through your artwork. With humor or sensitivity, your artwork can serve a purpose in someone else's life, and for that you can earn a good living.

Perhaps you prefer to work one on one with your customer, rather than dealing with corporate entities and mass-production techniques. This would involve creating a more personalized form of art such as jewelry or tattoos or pursuing one-of-a-kind commissions for individual clients such as murals, portraits, and sculptures. These forms of artwork serve a completely different market than the business-to-business and community-based artwork mentioned above. However, they are all *forms of service* that require a unique set of talents and creative abilities for which you can be paid. Remember, you do not get paid because you have talent; you get paid because you provide a service with your talent.

Marketing personalized artwork requires a different strategy than working with a repeat client. As an artist, you want to strike a balance between your head and your heart by spending your time creating things you enjoy and that have emotional meaning to you. At the same time, you understand that these things have to provide value to that particular segment of the marketplace that is willing to pay for the work you do.

The artist wants to create things that have *meaning*, and the marketplace wants to pay for things that have *value*. This is where we have to strike a balance between the emotional joy we feel when we are expressing ourselves and our intellectual ability to serve the needs of the customer so we can get paid. We need to be as smart as we are creative.

Any service of any kind has the potential for making money, but if you want to be in the business of selling your artwork, you must understand who your customer is and what that customer wants.

It's very likely that your perfect customer is very similar to you. Business-minded people are likely to relate to the needs of other businesses and then serve those needs because they understand those needs. Those of us who prefer to work on a more personal level with our customers are more likely to attract people like ourselves to our products and services because we have an unconscious understanding of each other, even before we meet. Birds of a feather tend to find each other, and with today's social media marketing techniques, connecting with your perfect market is easier and cheaper than ever before. Facebook refers to it as target marketing, and it's very effective.

Artists who enjoy creating jewelry tend to attract customers who like to wear jewelry. The same applies to artists who enjoy doing tattoos, attracting people who like tattoos. As artists, we tend to design things for ourselves that other people might like. Our own creations or expressions have to be self-satisfying and fun to do in order to keep us interested in the work, and they have to be customer satisfying in order for someone to be willing to pay for them.

If we are looking for steady creative work, it may be disappointing to find that the conventional job prospects for artists may be rather small, but it's important to remember that *the opportunities to be of service are unlimited.* Remember also that people pay for service, so the opportunities to earn money are also unlimited. I suggest that we stop looking for a job and focus instead on looking for opportunities to serve. Find ways to apply our chosen art form in ways that people enjoy and value.

Musicians and singers package their art with YouTube videos, digital downloads, and CDs. Storytellers use books, downloads, and podcasts, and some stories get turned into movies, which can then be sold in various forms. We always need to refer back to the thought of how the things we love to do can benefit the world and how we can package them in a way that they can be shared in the marketplace.

When we have something to offer and we make it available in a way that people can see what we are offering, those who are attracted to it will ask questions and make specific requests. These requests can set us on a new path that we might not take on our own, but the doors of opportunity continue to open for those who are ready and willing to walk through them. The opportunities to be of service are unlimited, and our success depends on our willingness to serve.

Besides the ability to earn money with our self-expression, another effect we might want our artwork to have would be as influential art. This type of art is not necessarily done with the intention of earning money as much as it's intended to make a statement, to inspire or influence someone's awareness or opinion. Graffiti falls into this category. It's hard to get paid for that kind of public artwork, but it certainly can have an effect on the community it serves. Some graffiti shows a high level of artistic skill, as it employs the power of the visual image. The message, the style, and the location all play a part in having an effect on the people who see it.

Public statues are another form of influential artwork.

Statues and sculptures are meant to have some kind of effect on their surroundings. Three-dimensional artwork is especially effective at silently affecting us on a subconscious and emotional level. Some artwork such as fountains and religious statues can have a pleasant and peaceful effect on their immediate surroundings, while other public statues such as the Statue of Liberty can influence the perspective and attitude of an entire nation and perhaps the entire world. Religious and political images are some of the oldest known forms of public artistic expression because of the powerful influence the image has on the minds of the people who see them.

As artists, we are dealing with powerful stuff. We are dealing with something that can bypass reason and logic and go straight to the heart of the matter. A visual image can cause people to see things and experience situations from a new perspective. The image can arouse emotions of anger or soothe the troubled spirit with peaceful and healing vibrations. Art is powerful, and as a professional artist, it's important to learn how to use it effectively.

What is the purpose of art in your life?

Ask yourself, "What value do I get from expressing myself? What is it that motivates me? Why do I want to express myself? What am I trying to say with my form of expression? What effect do I want to have on the world? What would I like to accomplish for myself with my talent?" These are important questions to answer, because the answers we come up with are what makes all the effort we go through worthwhile.

Being a professional artist and making a career out of using our talents requires a commitment to a lifetime of continually learning new things. Repetition is not creative. Being creative requires coming up with new ideas and products and making use of the new marketing techniques as technology and the social media platforms continue to evolve and new opportunities become possible. This is a great time to be creative!

Artwork can serve a purpose that is so much more than simple decoration, and the power we have to use it effectively is literally in our hands. The mind speaks in pictures. It's called psycho-pictography or mind pictures. It's our imagination, and it's how we communicate with each other through the use of the visual image. If I say the word *shoe,* you know what I mean. We may not imagine the same kind of shoe, but each of us creates some kind of image in our imagination when we hear the word *shoe,* and that makes it possible for us to communicate on some level. We can refine and share a more accurate concept of the word *shoe* by adding more specific details such as tennis shoe or red tennis shoe with white laces, etc.

The more I describe what I'm thinking about, the more we will imagine the same thing. However, if I just showed you a picture of a red tennis shoe with white laces, you would have immediately known what I was referring to without the use of any words at all. Art can be thought of as a tool. When we understand the truth behind the saying "a picture is worth a thousand words," we can learn how to have an instant impact on the public perception of things simply by using our talents and tools effectively. Art is a tool that we have at our disposal, and we can use it to achieve specific results.

Documentary films and photographs are very effective visual communicators, and they have the power to influence people's perceptions. Statues and paintings with religious themes and symbols have traditionally adorned the walls of homes, and they've had their silent effect on the hearts and minds of the occupants for generations.

Some of the earliest known artwork found in the caves of France depicts animals. It is possible that the cave had been used as a location for a public gathering or possibly as a place to prepare for a hunt. Some walls show scars of things striking the surface of the drawings, leading to the idea that the art was used as part of a prehunt ritual. The artwork appears to have served a purpose that was more important to their society than simply decorating the wall.

In the process of creating the drawings on the cave walls, the artists have unintentionally left their mark, and they have given us an opportunity to study and learn something about their culture at this later date. This is not a study in art history, but it's important to realize that when we participate in the activity of expressing ourselves creatively, we are contributing to the history of humanity. We are participating in the culture of our time, and by leaving our mark, we are potentially leaving something of value for future generations while we are personally working on ways to survive in this moment.

In this book, I want to focus on surviving in this moment. We'll leave long-term fame to the historians, since we're not likely to be around to enjoy it in the future anyway. In this book, we'll focus on ways to earn a living now, as we develop our reputations as artists in this lifetime. We need the money today, and when we learn how to apply our talents to the needs of others, the idea of the starving artist can be a thing of the past.

However, if instant fame is something you want in this lifetime, congratulations! It's never been easier to be famous than it is today. With social media and all the other ways of getting our message and our image out there, fame can be bought with enough advertising dollars. But is fame what we *really* want as an end in itself? If it is, then we need to focus our attention on promotion. Promotion and fame go hand in hand, but fame fades quickly if it's not constantly maintained.

Instead of focusing on the word *fame,* I prefer to focus on the idea of reputation. In today's business terms, it's called *branding.* We want to create a positive brand image for ourselves and our services and products, so that when people are thinking about something we offer, our name or brand comes to mind first.

There's a difference between promoting ourselves and creating a brand for ourselves, and we need to understand the difference between the two. We use promotion for the sake of making the public aware of our services and products, and we use branding as a way of intentionally shaping the public's image and perception of ourselves and our products. Both are important, and both work together to build our business.

When we have something to promote, such as a specific product or service or perhaps a special event or something that has a short term of opportunity, promotional advertising is needed to get the word out. If we're trying to establish ourselves as *the* particular person or business to call for specific things, that's an example of branding our image. Branding is more of a public relations activity than a promotional act. The effect of branding is meant to be long term, and the brand is built over time with repeated consistency. Also, branding (or our reputation) doesn't have an expiration date, while a promotion usually does.

There's a lot of power in having a marketable brand (think Apple), and when we are the name or brand that comes to mind first, our reputation is paying off. Obviously, it's important to build and maintain a good reputation in any business, and the creative industries are no different. Word-of-mouth advertising is still the best form of promotion, and with the help of Facebook and Google, the word of mouth can spread faster and further today than ever before. As a bonus, today, with the help of social media, we can help our reputation along with a few advertising dollars of our own, just to speed up the process of success.

A good reputation requires more than just a good product. A reputation is a long-term investment, and it has to be built and maintained every day. Our good reputation also requires all the other qualities we would expect from a professional business, such as prompt service, politeness, and neatness of appearance. We're still dealing with people, whether it's person to person or automated over the internet, and our marketing has to be geared toward treating others the way we want to be treated.

Now that we've discussed a little bit about the purpose art plays in society, on a more personal level, we need to understand what purpose art plays in our individual lives.

We need to ask ourselves some basic questions, such as: Should my talent be more than a hobby? Do I want to earn money with my talent? If I do artwork as a business, will it take the joy out of it? *(It doesn't have to.)* Would I prefer to earn money by using my talents, or would I prefer to do whatever I am doing now? Do I prefer to work as part of a team or more independently and on my own?

These are the kind of questions we can only answer for ourselves. But it's important to remember, each of us can create the life we can imagine. Whatever we believe to be true becomes possible because our imaginations and our beliefs determine the direction we take our lives. Just as we can imagine and then create an art object, we can use the same process to imagine and then create an entire lifestyle for ourselves.

Finding Purpose

So, how do we know what our purpose is? The answer is found in how we feel. We all come here with lessons to learn, and we all have gifts to offer. If we use our gifts, we will learn our lessons, and life will become a series of fascinating events and be very meaningful for us. If we don't use our gifts, we may find ways to earn an income, but we will have a hard time finding the satisfaction we desire for a happy and fulfilling life.

The recipe for a happy and fulfilling life requires balancing our physical health with our mental ability to earn a satisfactory income, while we express ourselves emotionally and fulfill our sense of purpose in the process. For a fulfilling life, boredom is not an option.

It's safe to say that we are all here to serve in some way. If we follow our hearts or our intuition, we will be guided to see and do things that make us feel good on a deep inner level. It's that feeling we get when we know we're doing the right thing, regardless of what others may suggest or consider to be practical. Hopefully, we can be guided to listen to our hearts and to get to know that deep inner part of us at an early age, while our imaginations are still wide open and our hearts haven't been covered with the concerns for all the outer distractions.

That voice is our conscience or inner guide telling us that "this is the way to go," or "that's not what you really want to be doing." Listening to this voice or inner urge and following our intuitive feeling will lead us on a path that is uniquely our own.

Remember, we may not always have a job, but we always have a purpose, and if we know what our purpose is, then our job is to fulfill our purpose.

Having a sense of purpose is essential to having a sense of fulfillment, so let's think about what it takes to feel fulfilled in the work we do. Having a sense of fulfillment will be different for each of us. No two people have the same gifts to work with, and no two people have the same lessons to learn. No two people have the same level of ambition or the same challenges that need to be satisfied. No two people have the exact same market to serve nor do they have the same way of serving that market, and in that way, we are each unique.

We each have our own style, and that is our distinguishing feature that we offer to the world. Our style is a recognizable part of our signature, and it should be distinctive. Our unique style is the element that sets us apart from everyone else in the same industry. There is no need to copy someone else's style, but of course, we are always being influenced by the things we see around us. We gladly absorb elements from the people and things we enjoy.

Ask yourself, "What difference do *I* want to make in the world and in the particular market I choose to serve?" What effect do I want to have on the audience I'm reaching for? What kind of people do I most enjoy working with and working for?

Write it down! Start to make a list of the things you enjoy doing. Lists are very important for achieving specific goals. Lists become the maps we follow and use to mark our progress on a daily, yearly, and lifetime process. I suggest you make several lists for various categories as we continue to grow throughout our lives and our careers. Lists help to focus our attention on specific short-term goals, as well as stretching our imaginations to see the long-term end result we want. Lists keep things on track, and they become the blueprints for what we intend to accomplish daily and in a lifetime.

The benefit of understanding our purpose for doing the work we enjoy is that it elevates our activities from being a job into being a mission. Being on a mission is more than just trying to earn money. Being on a mission is being inspired to leave our mark and to make a difference in the world.

In summary of this chapter, I'd like to leave you with the understanding that we all have a purpose for being here, and we've all been given gifts or talents to use while we're here. For every one of us, our purpose is to serve others in some way, so we might as well use the unique gifts we've been given as our way to serve the needs of those people. Since we understand that people are willing to pay for things that serve their needs, we can find ways to earn a living for ourselves by giving of ourselves. It's a wonderful cycle of giving and receiving that keeps us in harmony with the natural patterns of life while we pursue and fulfill our own personal needs and interests.

Chapter 3

CREATING THE MASTERPIECE

In order to create a masterpiece, the artist must first be a master.

There's more to our need for self-expression than what meets the eye. We know things can have a deeper meaning than how they appear on the surface. As human beings, we are more than just separate physical bodies walking around on this planet. We all share the same emotions, and even though we express them at different times and for different reasons, we have the same inventory of feelings we can choose to express, at least until we learn to shut them off or we let them run out of control. All forms of art communicate on multiple levels, and art affects different people differently. People see and hear things at whatever level of awareness they are in harmony with. That's how we relate to each other, and that's how we attract the people we want in our lives, either as partners or as customers.

Our level of awareness about a subject determines what we can express about that subject. We can only give what we have, and we can't give something we don't have. So, let's start with a very interesting perspective on who we are as human beings, and then we can learn new and powerful ways to use the creative gifts we have been given.

We all have four essential elements that make us human: our physical bodies, our emotional feelings, our intellectual thinking abilities, and the power of being alive—the power that beats our hearts and animates our bodies. Without that fourth element, the power of life itself, the other three don't matter. When we recognize each of these elements as being distinctly different from each other but realize how they are interconnected within our own selves, we will see them in everyone else as well. We all have these four elements, and we can connect with people on each of these levels. The awareness of this fact can broaden our relationships with people immensely.

It's likely that we have all enjoyed a good intellectual relationship with someone at some point, perhaps with a friend or a teacher, when we shared ideas and enjoyed conversations together. We can have a pleasant intellectual relationship with someone even though we've never physically met. We might just read their books or enjoy talking to them online or on the phone, but intellectually a sort of bond gets established. We've also had emotional relationships with friends, family members, and pets. Physical relationships occur every time we meet someone in a specific location. These experiences are all transitory in the sense that we aren't constantly engaged with other people, but we are constantly alive.

The power of being alive is one thing we share. We have our individual bodies, and we express our personal emotions, and we come up with our own intellectual solutions to problems, but the one thing everyone has in common is that our bodies and minds are being powered by some invisible force we refer to as "life." Even though no one can say exactly where it's located, we all have it.

This power we think of as the lifeforce within us is the same life that's in all living things including plants and animals, insects, bacteria, and anything else that is alive. All living things share that invisible lifeforce, but it's impossible to locate it in any one place.

For example, if a plant is alive and we want to locate the source of its aliveness, we might cut it open to search for it, but we won't be able to locate exactly where the lifeforce is, because it's in every individual cell that makes up the plant, and it's active throughout the entire form of the complete plant. In the process of searching for a specific place where life is located, we end up destroying the physical form of the living thing, and we're still unable to determine the exact location of the lifeforce, because it is everywhere but nowhere specifically. Still, we know that the power of life is real because we're experiencing it in our own lives at every moment, even though we can't pinpoint its exact location within ourselves either.

The important thing to realize is that we are *alive,* and as long as that power of life is flowing through our hearts (emotions), our minds (our intellect), and our bodies (the physical part of us), we are complete. We have all the tools we need to survive and prosper. But without that energy of life, our bodies won't function, even though all the physical parts are still there; our minds won't think, and our emotions won't matter much either. It takes all four elements working together to be a complete person.

It's important to recognize that as individuals, we are the alive part of the equation. Our personal thoughts and our individual feelings depend on that living part of us for their existence. Even the physical part of us is dependent on the power of life for its continued existence. Once that lifeforce abandons the body, it tends to deteriorate quickly.

So, what does all of this have to do with earning money with our artwork? As businesspeople, it's helpful to understand how each of these elements works in harmony with each other and to recognize that these four elements show up in every situation we find ourselves in. When it comes to marketing our services and products, there is a specific pattern that takes place in every transaction, and it involves all four of the elements of being human.

Every activity we participate in involves us as whole people, though we may not be aware of it. Most people aren't. I want this chapter to be about raising our personal awareness of how each of these elements is interacting within us every day and in every situation of our lives. With this increased awareness, we can learn how to become more effective in our communication with others, and that is what our self-expression or artwork is all about. We are trying to express ourselves in some creative fashion in order to communicate something to the world. As artists, we have something to say, or we have a unique way of saying it on behalf of our clients. Art is all about communicating an idea, and any improvement in our communication skills can create more effective results in sales, which in turn will result in an increased income.

As long as we are alive, our minds, our emotions, and our bodies react constantly to the stimulation of the world around us. We are constantly being bombarded with noise and visual things that impact our senses, and we must constantly tune some of it out and consciously choose to pay attention to other things. We are constantly engaging and interacting with our surroundings and the people we meet, and our interactions affect us on many levels.

For example, when we first encounter a person, we see him

or her physically as another person with a physical form, but then we immediately get some sort of emotional reaction. If it's a simple encounter of walking toward someone on the street, the emotional reaction is usually one of caution mixed with a touch of friendliness or a touch of fear. Either way, the *physical* encounter has caused an *emotional* reaction, which then triggers an *intellectual* decision to either continue along our path or perhaps cross the street to the other side.

All of this can only happen because we have that fourth element of *life* operating within us. Without that element of life, none of the other stuff matters because we wouldn't exist anymore, at least not in our physical form. It's important to remain aware that the power of being alive is the ultimate power for getting anything done, and each of us has that power given to us at birth.

With proper instruction and motivation, everyone can use the power of being alive to their advantage by developing various ways to serve others, and they will prosper themselves accordingly. The key to prosperity for each of us is found in how we use our imaginations and how we apply them to create real-world solutions that effectively serve the needs of others. Let's study how the four elements work together to make a successful sales experience for both the artist and the client.

At some point, there is a physical meeting between the client and the artist. This is essentially a sales presentation. Perhaps it's at an open-air art show, or it may be done as an interview with a gallery owner in an office or even online at the home of the client. Regardless of the physical location, we want the client to be *physically comfortable,* so their attention can be on our product and our message and not on their discomfort. So, to set up a successful sales situation, step one is to make sure the client is in a physically and emotionally comfortable environment.

In step two, we want to engage them intellectually. We want to get their attention by offering them something that will interest them and be of value to them. We can grab their attention with a bold headline or bright colors that catch their eye or show them something that moves and glitters and so forth. If we're able to capture their intellectual interest or curiosity, they will at least look at our product and be able to consider its value. If we are unable to catch their attention in the first place, we won't be able to engage them intellectually, and we won't arouse their emotional desire to want what we are offering. When that happens, they will not benefit from our service, and we won't benefit from the sale.

If we're on a mission to make a difference and we want to have a positive effect on the lives of our community, *we owe it* to the marketplace to make them aware of how our products and services can improve their lives. Remember, we are not asking anyone for anything; instead, we are offering our services in the hopes of making someone else's life better.

We are all here to be of service to others in some way, and when we choose to serve our community with our creative talents, we are choosing to use our unique skills as our way of doing for others what they can't do for themselves. We are using our chosen form of self-expression to improve the lives of others in some artistic way.

Once we have captured our client's attention, step three is to engage them emotionally with the feeling of desire. We need to get them emotionally excited to the point that they want what we are offering. People have to desire something before they become willing to pay for it.

People buy things emotionally; then they figure out intellectually how they're going to pay for them. They already bought it in their mind and for them it's really just a matter of justifying the cost or figuring out where to put it and so forth. Our emotions trigger our intellect, and our intellect is left with the job of finding the solutions.

At this point, we've met our client physically, we've engaged them intellectually, and we've gotten them excited about what we are offering. Now it's that fourth element of being alive that makes this whole exchange of talent for money possible. In the process of exchanging something that we have created for something the customer values (usually money), we have completed the cycle of giving and receiving, serving the needs of others while fulfilling the purpose for which we were born.

The apple tree produces apples, but it has no use for the apples it produces, but still, it needs to continue to produce its fruit or it will die. As creative people, we need to continue to make use of our unique gifts or they too will wither and die. Our bodies may continue to walk around on this planet and even earn a substantial income in an unrelated career, but that creative, imaginative and passionate part of us will have died or at least gotten buried somewhere in the everyday shuffle of paying the bills.

Investing in our talents is the best investment we can make. In the physical world, the more we use something, the more it wears out, and eventually it needs to be replaced. However, in the world of the imagination, the more we use it, the more it expands, and the stronger it becomes.

When we make use of our talents, we exercise our "creative muscle," and the more we use it, the stronger it gets. Imagination is the infinite well from which anything can be created. The more we use our imaginations, the more we realize there is no limit to what we can imagine. *Imagine that!*

Here's a simple formula for creating anything we want:

Imagination + Belief = Having.

There's a familiar phrase that says, "as you believe, so shall it be," or a similar one that says, "as a man thinks in his heart, so is he." These sayings point to the fact that we create our version of reality with the power of our beliefs. If we believe in the things that we imagine and we imagine the things that we want, we empower ourselves to create and have the things we desire. The more we practice our craft, the more we will discover about ourselves. The more we discover, the more we become able to do new things, and the cycle continues to grow. Without a doubt, we are our own best investment.

Investing in our imagination is a cumulative investment that can pay dividends immediately while it continues to expand for as long as we live. Our imagination and what we choose to do with it can feed us today, and it can leave an impression long after we're gone. Our life's work is our legacy.

This pattern of our four aspects progressing from the physical encounter into an intellectual interest, then growing into an emotional desire, and finally consummating with the exchange of something each participant values, goes on constantly. I want to show a few examples of how this pattern plays out over and over in our everyday lives for the purpose of being aware of the pattern, so we can intentionally incorporate it into our marketing.

Example 1, the phone call:

The phone rings. We react by being intellectually curious about who's calling. We physically reach for the phone, pick it up to see whose name or number appears, and when we see it, we get some kind of emotional reaction.

If it's a friend, we get a certain feeling of comfort, but if it's a person we don't want to speak with, we get a completely different emotional reaction. When we answer the phone and receive the message, we have completed the cycle. In this simple example, I have demonstrated that a simple ring of a telephone will cause a physical and emotional reaction that results in an intellectual decision to answer or ignore the phone call. All of this happens because the power of being alive is active within us, and we are able to react to outside stimulation.

Example 2, the rock concert:

If you've been to a rock concert, you will notice a specific pattern to the evening's presentation. Before the band comes out on stage, background music is played to set the mood for the evening's performance. This creates an atmosphere of physical comfort mixed with emotional anticipation. When the concert begins, the band starts by performing some of their familiar hits. This has the effect of making us emotionally comfortable by reassuring us that we're going to hear the songs we wanted to hear.

Once the performers have made us comfortable with a few familiar songs, phase two, the intellectual phase, kicks in, and it sounds like this: "We'd like to play something off of our latest album for you."

Playing the new songs engages our intellect, as we now have to think about how to process this new material. We make quick decisions about whether we like it or not and if it fits in with what we've come to expect from the band. When something is new, we have to think about what we want to do with it, and we make decisions about how we want to react to it. We can accept it or reject it. It's our decision, and we're making these kinds of choices constantly.

The third phase of a rock concert is the emotional part, where the audience pulls out their cell phones and waves them back and forth in the air as they sway to a song that has a meaningful message. From there, the band glides smoothly into the fourth phase.

The fourth phase begins as the band heads toward the big finale and the lead singer tells the audience to "put your hands together." Everyone starts to clap to the beat of the music and sing along to the same words, and the whole room participates in the experience of one rhythm, one sound, and one feeling, if only for a short time.

Example 3, *The Wizard of Oz*

We're all familiar with the story of *The Wizard of Oz* and the four main characters who went on a journey in search of the Wizard, so he could help them get the things they wanted most in life. The Scarecrow wanted a brain (the intellect), the Tin Man wanted a heart (the emotions), the Lion wanted courage (physical strength), and Dorothy wanted to get back home to where she was meant to be.

We all want to feel like we're where we belong. That's *our* story in a nutshell. *The Wizard of Oz* is the story of each of our lives as we can see ourselves in each of the characters' longing for something they already possess but don't know it.

If you're not familiar with the story, please get a copy of the movie and watch it. It's as classic as *Aesop's Fables* and Greek mythology because it addresses the universal truths about our human nature.

Without retelling the whole story, let me summarize the gist of the message. Dorothy gets hit on the head during a tornado, and she has a dream. In the dream, she is in a strange land and she wants to get back to Kansas. She meets a scarecrow who is upset because he doesn't have a brain in his head, so the two of them go in search of the Wizard, who they think can give them what they lack. Along the way, they meet a tin man who is crying because he doesn't have a heart, so the three of them continue on the journey to find the Wizard. They meet up with a cowardly lion who has no courage and can't scare anyone, so he joins the other three in hopes that the Wizard can help him be strong and courageous.

While on their journey, they encounter all sorts of obstacles, and Dorothy is taken prisoner in the witch's castle. The Scarecrow figures out a plan where the Lion is able to courageously sneak into the castle and makes it possible for the Tin Man to chop through the prison door to free Dorothy.

Dorothy escapes, and they continue on their journey to see if the Wizard can help them, only to find out that the Wizard is a phony, just an ordinary guy behind the curtain. They learn that they didn't need anyone like him anyway, because they (we) already had everything they wanted, even before they went on their journey. The only thing they didn't have was awareness.

The Scarecrow had the brains to figure out how to get

Dorothy out of the castle. The Lion had the courage to sneak into the castle with the flying monkey guards, and the Tin Man was crying because he didn't have a heart (but you can't cry if you don't have feelings). Dorothy was never lost, because she never left her home. She was only having a dream.

We are all where we belong all the time! We already have within us everything we seek as we go on our own life's journey. The question is, do we realize that, and what are we going to do about it now that we're here? I simply suggest that we make the most of it.

Chapter 4

THE KEYS TO HAPPINESS AND THE KEYS TO SUCCESS

As artists, we understand that our imagination is the greatest tool we have to help us shape the world as we want it to be. If we can't make the entire world the way we want it to be, at least we can imagine the part that we want to contribute. Our self-expression is our contribution to the world.

We can't give what we don't have, so it's important for us to be clear about what we are offering to the world. To do that, it's important to take stock of our personal creative inventory and expand it if necessary, through further education, letting go of old ideas and enhancing our attitudes for success with good business habits. A lifetime of personal development will lead to greater influence (sales) in the marketplace, and the more we sell, the more our artwork can influence the world we live in. The more we sell, the more money we can earn as a result of sharing ourselves with the world. Sales are a good indicator that we are doing something right.

Many talented people prefer to keep their talent to themselves, and they prefer to use it only for their personal relaxation and enjoyment, such as singing in the shower, painting once in a while, or making small gift items for friends. That's a perfectly fine way to make use of our talents if we want to enjoy them only as a hobby, but if we want to earn a living with our talents, we must be willing to share our gifts with the world. The more successful we are at developing and sharing our unique gifts, the better off the world will be, and the more money we are likely to earn in return. It's a win-win relationship when everyone gets something of value.

I'm going to assume that we want to earn money with the way we express ourselves and consequently, we want the work that we do to be enjoyed and appreciated by others. People are happy to spend money on things they enjoy. For me, that's what it's all about, having a positive effect on the lives of the people who experience my artwork. I want my work to make a positive contribution to the community I live in, whether it's a commercial sign painted for a business or a landscape mural painted in someone's backyard. My intention is always to make a situation more beautiful than it was before I arrived. My mission in life is to make this world a more beautiful place for people to live and work in, and I get that opportunity every day. In that sense, I have job security because I'll never run out of things to do.

As artists, we use our self-expression to share our personal feelings with the world. We put our hearts into the things we do. We're passionate about the things we believe in, and we have a strong urge to tell the world about it. We pack our emotions into the words of a song or the subject of a painting. We might make a video or a sculpture, or perhaps we create an image for a tattoo or shape a piece of metal into a beautiful piece of jewelry. We all have our favorite way of expressing ourselves, and what we do isn't as important as why we do it. Whatever our personal motivation is, as artists, we focus our emotions and concentrate them into a passionate expression that others can see and feel when they experience our work. People who relate to the work will be attracted to it, and some of those people will be eager to purchase it if it's in a marketable form.

People are more willing to spend money on things that excite them and make them feel good than they are eager to part with their money for something that displeases them or is forced onto them, such as an unexpected repair bill. That suggests that we might want to focus our creative expression toward things people want and enjoy. While we all have the freedom to choose what we want to say and how we want to say it, we can't help but express what we *are* in the process, because what we are is all we really have to offer. We can't offer something that we are not, but we can develop within ourselves whatever it is we want to offer, even if we don't have that quality now. The seed of wanting something is the starting point of getting something, and that's where the journey of self-discovery and development begins.

We might offer beauty or humor through our art. We may rely on cleverness or trending social events for inspiration. Whatever we do, our art is more than the image we see with our eyes. Our art also includes the invisible power it has on the mind of the beholder. Does it soothe or heal the spirit? Does it excite the potential buyer into wanting the product that's shown in the artwork? Artwork as a commercial tool has been used for centuries to cause an effect on the people who experience it. Commercial artwork that is used for advertising is an example of artwork at work. It's not meant to be decorative. It's meant to be seen, and it's meant to have a particular effect.

Lighting and camera angles, backdrop scenery, and so forth are all artistic elements that work together to get a particular result. The artistic image can be powerful, and as a professional artist, you will learn how to handle it well. Much more subtle messages can be conveyed through the effective use of artwork than many other forms of media.

We can express our anger, if that's what we're feeling, but will the marketplace want to buy it? Perhaps, if we package it as angry rock music or in the form of a social documentary. Political satire and Hollywood-style movies can convey angry emotions in a manner that the public can consume as well. A single eye-catching word or symbol printed on a t-shirt can be worn in public as a statement or a personal commentary. There's a market for anything if it's packaged and presented in a form that can be bought and sold. The big question is always, what do we want *our* contribution to be, and how do we want to leave our mark?

Whenever we promote our product or service, we are constantly adding to our public image, as we build a portfolio of things we've done. We're creating a public image or reputation for ourselves to live up to, and our image is based on more than a single product. It's important to think long term. Living the life of an artist is a lifelong personal journey of self-discovery and expression. It will lead each of us on our own fascinating path, which will be different than anyone else's path, and it offers us an adventure we don't want to miss. It is literally the adventure of a lifetime!

As professional businesspeople, we want our business to continually grow and continue to improve for as long as we are actively producing artwork. To do that, we want a style of expression that has the potential for continued growth and offers us an abundance of interesting opportunities to keep ourselves fascinated with the work we do. Boredom is not an option.

While the expression of anger may be a valid emotional experience, and there are some very creative ways to channel that anger and get paid for it, there's only so far that it can go without becoming destructive. At some point, the expression of anger has to cool off, or its expansion will eventually be like a cancer that destroys its own success.

It's good to remember that people actually enjoy paying for things that make them feel good, so I suggest that if we want a long-lasting and positive return on our investment of time and effort, we should focus our creativity on things that make ourselves, our communities, and other people feel good. In doing so, we will be lending a hand in making the world a better place, and we will be getting paid to do it.

Artwork can be enjoyed by the artist for as many reasons as there are artists. It can be therapeutic and relaxing for some and educational and challenging for others. Our imaginations are ours to do with what we want, and we all have something to say. Our personal responsibility is to decide how we want to use our imaginations and what form of expression we want to use as our way of sharing it.

The pursuit of happiness is an inner search-and-discovery adventure. Happiness doesn't exist outside of us. Happiness is not a tangible thing that someone can find sitting in a specific location or caused by a specific situation. Our happiness is something that we have to create from within us, like any other work of art. Happiness is an attitude. Attitudes are things we carry with us wherever we go, and we are expressing our attitude whenever we produce our artwork. To a large degree, we use our attitude to define who we think we are and how we want the public to perceive us. Our personal attitude shows up in our artwork. Is it irreverent? Is it humorous? Is it beautiful? Whatever quality it expresses, it is a reflection of the artist's attitude.

For some of us, learning to control our attitude may be the biggest challenge we face as human beings, and it can be especially challenging in business situations. We're all familiar with the common statement, "I can't help it; that's just the way I am!" While this position of helplessness may be adequate for some people, the creative person who understands the power of the imagination knows that we can change our lives by changing our attitude. This can be done by changing the pictures we hold in our imaginations.

Let's do a quick and simple test right now. Take a moment to visualize an image or a situation where you were upset about something. Any example will work. Imagine yourself in that situation of upset, and assess how you feel emotionally. Stay with that vision for a moment and really feel it; then change your image to something enjoyable and pleasant. Assess your feelings now. Spend enough time with the vision to allow yourself to feel the shift from one emotion to another. Notice the effect each vision has on your emotions. Do the same exercise with images that excite you, taking time to feel the effect the image has on your emotions; then spend time with images that relax you. Realize for yourself how the images you hold in your imagination affect how you feel at any given moment, and realize that our images can have that kind of effect on the people who experience our art. Every image has power, and as artists, we get to decide how we want to apply it.

All people create for themselves the things they believe to

be true. There are some people who seem to be born happy; there are others who seem to spend their lives in perpetual misery. Since I'm not a psychologist, I won't even pretend to have any professional insights, but I will offer my humble personal opinion from my own experience.

I know I'm happiest when I think happy thoughts, and I know I feel miserable, or at least less enthusiastic about everything, when I dwell on unpleasant topics. Therein lies the key. *Happiness is to be found in the thoughts we choose to think.*

As artists, we are aware that we use our imaginations to visualize our next project or to determine the next stroke of the brush that's needed to make something just right. We are aware that we use the power of the imagination in very intentional ways in order to create the end results we want. We can apply this power of the imagination to any aspect of our lives that needs attention, and consequently, we have the power to create the kind of life we want for ourselves. Our entire lives are a work of art.

Everyone can control their thoughts, but it does take effort to learn how it's done. In the same way we dedicate ourselves to working out at a gymnasium in order to build stronger and healthier muscles, it takes a focused and committed effort to consciously choose what thoughts we want to think and dwell on. The mind speaks in pictures, and when we understand that, we have the key to putting the power of the image to work for us. In order to stay on track with our goals or to make changes in our lives, we need to respect the power of our own imagination, and we need to be aware of the pictures we run through our mental screen and realize how they are affecting us every day of our lives.

The artistic person is blessed with a conscious awareness

that the imagination is just as real as the physical world that surrounds us. As artists, we value our imaginations, and we understand that whatever kinds of things we imagine today could become a part of the physical world through our artistic efforts. We know how to imagine a sculpture or a piece of jewelry, or how we want a painting to end up before we even get started. We might use our imaginations to sketch something on paper in order to gain clarity or to share the idea with someone else. The sketch becomes a visual blueprint for something that at the moment only exists in our imagination.

All people use their imaginations to create their everyday experiences, but as artists, we use our imaginations to see new things. Others use their imaginations to see the same things over and over every day of their lives, and then they say they have no imagination. They have just as much imagination as anyone else; they simply limit their mental images to things that they are familiar with. Consequently, by not imagining anything new, they create and repeat the same experiences over and over again.

They believe that they have no imagination, while the reality is that they have no new images to imagine. It's actually their imagination that's locking them into their perpetual repetition. The creative power is still working twenty-four hours each day, but it's creating the repetitive results we get when we imagine the same series of activities every day, over and over again. While many people may consider that to be a form of security or stability, the creative person will find it to be boring.

Creativity is adventurous. It requires going places no one has gone before and doing things we haven't already experienced, trying new combinations of things that interest us, and being willing to fail at getting the results we want but realizing that we learned something in the process. Creativity is fun and exciting, and our self-expression is our natural way of discovering who we really are. It's our way of sharing ourselves with the world.

The key to happiness is to figure out what we like to do and then find a way to get paid to do it.

The key to success is that we can do anything we want to do, as long as we do it in a way that benefits others.

People don't pay us for what we do; they pay us for the benefit they get from the work we do. So, let's do the world a favor and use our talents to do great things.

Chapter 5

TALENT AND CURIOSITY

We know we have talent, but what is it really? Is it a gift that some have been blessed with and others have not? I don't think so. Talents are developed as a result of being interested in a subject enough that we understand the fundamental aspects and master the skills associated with it.

No one is born with talent, but we're all born with a natural curiosity about things. We want to climb out of our cribs and crawl around corners to see what's on the other side. We want to climb on ladders and do dangerous things because we don't realize that they are dangerous, and we have no fear.

When we are very young, we haven't yet learned what we shouldn't be doing. We have a natural curiosity, and God bless the parents and teachers who encourage us to use it. Talent thrives on curiosity. It's important to keep that childlike amazement of discovery in everything we do. Constantly learning new things and making new discoveries keeps us interested in our work, and being creative people, interesting work is often more important to us than the financial rewards that are offered.

Talent is simply a personal interest in something that has

been developed into a skill, to a point where other people take notice of it. They recognize that our skills are above average, and *they* label us as being talented. The talented person doesn't always recognize him- or herself as being talented. For us, it's normal to think the way we think, and we're more concerned with our daily issues of survival than we are about our special gifts and talents. We often take our talents for granted, and we don't appreciate them sufficiently for what they have to offer in terms of wonderful products for others and inner satisfaction for ourselves.

When we get wrapped up in paying our bills and meeting our social obligations, we can easily forget to honor that creative spirit within us. That unique part of us needs to be recognized and encouraged for it to grow and stay healthy. There's a very real part of us that wants to be set free and desires to express itself in some way. You may be familiar with the phrase, "don't die with your music still in you." It's there, and we need to find creative ways to let it out.

There are a few distinct times in our lives when that inner urge calls out more loudly than others, and it's important that we respond to it in some way, or we will let that creative urge die from neglect as it retreats into the back of our minds. One of the first times this creative urge speaks loudly to us is about the age of ten to fifteen. At that age we're still young and discovering specific things that interest us, and we're still open to big dreams and the possibility of greatness. As children, we usually don't meet a lot of resistance when we talk about our childlike dreams and wishes. Anything is possible at that age, and if it's encouraged, it's likely that it will grow into something greater than average.

Another time we tend to make life-altering decisions is

around high school graduation. That's a critical time to decide on career choices and make serious plans. Another common cycle we go through is the so-called midlife crisis that seems to appear around the age of thirty or after we've been in our first career for about ten years and we're no longer feeling satisfied.

It's at these moments that we come to a fork in the road. We have to make a life-altering decision whether to honor our talents and see where they take us or to ignore that urge and play it safe. When we play it safe, we ignore the potential of our talents and we relegate them to the back of our priorities as we seek a more conventional but often less satisfying lifestyle.

There's more to a career than just earning a paycheck or having a (false) sense of job security. A good job or career also needs to offer an intellectual challenge that rewards our curiosity and keeps us excited about our work. No one pursues a career hoping that it will be a boring job. As creative people, we *want* to use our brains. We enjoy the creative challenge, and we appreciate the connection it gives us to something greater than ourselves.

Job security often leads to stagnation of the imagination. Routine and repetition kill creativity. The two concepts are at odds with each other. We either seek the adventure that comes with uncertainty and creativity by constantly trying new things, or we seek a false sense of security that comes with a steady job. But in today's changing world of technology and other related trends, job security is a thing of the past. A sense of job security today can only come from our willingness to be of service to others and by applying our personal creativity to the needs of the moment. There's always a market for those of us who can serve the needs of others. The trick is being able to satisfy ourselves in the process. Remember, we may not always have a job, but we always have a purpose.

No one does things exactly the same way as another person would do them, and no one sees things exactly the same way as others do. This is where our personal style begins to emerge and we set ourselves apart from everyone else stylistically, even though we may be engaged in the same industry or doing the same type of work. Whatever we do, it won't be exactly like anyone else's. There is no need to imitate others. Instead, we want to emulate their achievements and learn from what they have done. We want to figure out how they did it, but we do not want to copy or imitate them. Whoever "they" are, they had their lessons to learn, and they had their unique gifts to offer. Now it's our day, and our situation is different, so it's time for us to use our gifts, and we will learn our lessons in the process.

Each of us has our own reasons for wanting to express ourselves, and each of us has our own lessons to learn and our own ways of doing things. We develop our own style of expression based on our environmental and emotional influences, as well as the tools we have at our disposal and the materials we enjoy working with.

Our survival as artists depends on creatively using the things we have available to us and applying them to the needs of the market we want to serve. With today's target marketing technology offered by Facebook and similar platforms, it's easier than ever for artists to pick and choose our preferred audience. We can even show them pictures of what we have to offer without either of us ever leaving home. The challenge for each of us comes down to the question of what kinds of things do I enjoy making that the marketplace would value and consequently be willing to pay for? Another way of asking that question is, "Given the tools and materials I like to use, *what can I do for you?*"

The success of any business comes down to those six magic words: "How can I be of service?" or "What can I do for you?" How can I use my talents and do the things that I enjoy doing in such a way that it will serve the needs and interests of someone else? I can please myself simply with the joy I find in using my talent, but I can't expect to get paid if I'm my own client. Other people have to find value in the work we do if we expect them to pay for it.

We are all here to be of service in some way, and with the free will we've been given, we can choose how we want to serve others. No one can force us to be artists; we must make that choice for ourselves, but as artists we've been given something unique to offer to the public, and it would be a shame to waste that opportunity. If we don't offer our unique gifts, we will not benefit from the personal growth opportunity it represents, and the world will not benefit from the products or services we could be providing. Win-win is still the guiding principle of a long-term successful business, as well as an overall successful and fulfilling life.

Keep in mind that no one pays us for being talented. They pay us for *providing a service* with our talent. However, if the service we provide involves one or more of our talents, we will probably enjoy the work we do, we will do good work because we enjoy what we are doing, and we will earn good money because we do good work. But we are not getting paid just because we have talent; we are getting paid because we are benefitting someone with it in some way. For us to succeed, we must stay focused on how our service can benefit others. The biggest benefit to us is that we are fulfilling our mission in life.

The money is the reward for a job well done. Fulfillment is the reward for a life well lived. Both are necessary for a happy life.

Talent thrives on a healthy curiosity and a desire to constantly learn more and to *be* more. We live in a world that is filled with wonder like no other time has ever enjoyed. Whether it's the interconnectedness of the world through technology or the depth of understanding and simplified learning that's available to the average person with a computer, these days offer us so much to be excited about that it's easy to maintain a childlike fascination about the world. The more we learn, the more we realize there is to learn, and that's why we have curiosity.

Chapter 6

COURAGE AND CONFIDENCE

The definition of courage is *the ability to do something that frightens you.*

The definition of confidence is *a feeling of self-assurance arising from one's appreciation of one's own abilities or qualities.*

Courage is necessary to develop the confidence that is needed when we are starting any endeavor, because there are no guarantees, but that's the adventure of it all. To live an exciting life that fulfills the very reason why we are here requires that we have the courage to trust in something we don't understand, but we have a sense that it is guiding us in some way. It's that intuitive part of us that makes us feel like we're supposed to be doing something. Whatever we're doing with our lives right now either feels good or it doesn't feel right.

Confidence comes from trusting in ourselves and in our ability to make good decisions. Making good decisions requires us to trust in that inner guide or voice and to follow that intuitive feeling, even when the going gets rough and life's situations are challenging and we find ourselves asking, "Why am doing this?" The answer is that it feels right, whatever that means to you. There's something inside our heads and our hearts that tells us to keep on keeping on because this is what we are meant to be doing. We must listen to it and trust its guidance. The times that we face tough decisions are the times when we need to have the courage to take the next step and not retreat into safety out of fear. That voice or feeling is telling us something if we know how to listen. It would be a mistake to ignore it.

Life may seem very discouraging at times, and sometimes it may seem pointless to go on, but those moments give us the opportunity to reassess our thinking. We can make changes where necessary if something is out of balance or perhaps just out of date. It's possible that we've simply outgrown a period in our lives, and the things that were right for us in the past are no longer right for us. We've changed, and things around us have changed. There's no way of stopping that process, so the solution is to learn to live with it by adapting to the flow. It's part of growing up. To sit idly by as the world changes around us is to be left behind in a world that no longer exists. Things are constantly changing, and we must be able to go with the flow of the times while still maintaining our individual ethics, morals, and values.

In any epic story of the hero's journey, these moments represent the time of transition from innocence to greatness for the main character, which in this case is you. These are the forks in the road when we need to make an adjustment in some part of our thinking. This will require deciding to either take the road less traveled and follow our own unique path in life or to follow a more conventional path, though conventional paths are becoming less conventional every day.

Everyone faces moments of crisis at one time or another, and they give us a chance to adjust our perspective on what we are doing and what we are offering to the world. It's an opportunity to assess how well we are serving the needs of others. Always bear in mind that we are all here to serve in some way, and serving others in some way is the only way to get paid. So, let's start by making an inventory of what we currently have to offer, then figure out a way to deliver it to the public. Another way of saying it is, let's start by consulting our hearts to understand what excites us, and then we can engage our intellect to figure out how to get from where we are now to where we want to be. When we know what we want, we can follow our hearts and let the brain figure out the next steps as we trust that creative urge to guide us along the way.

There are always ways to improve the return on our investment of time, money, and effort by improving the quality of our service or product. This can be done by upgrading the materials and equipment we use to produce a better product and by improving the appearance of our presentation, from our website to our packaging to our personal appearance. It all works together as part of our marketing and public branding. The success of any business is in expanding and improving on what we are already doing. Think of Apple and how that company began. They started with a computer, they improved on that while they came up with a pocket-sized music player that could hold a thousand songs in your pocket. Then they added a phone and a camera and a few other things, and they still keep improving their products and their presentation. Success is an ever-expanding way of life that we can enjoy because there are no limits. We can stop anytime, but most creative people never want to.

In the beginning of any endeavor, it's not what we earn as much as what we learn that matters. The money comes and the money goes, but the lessons are ours to keep. By learning our lessons, we develop the confidence to put new ideas, tools, and habits into use in new and exciting ways. Our sense of confidence grows when we have positive experiences and gain positive reinforcement from the results. But before we can achieve a high level of confidence, we need to have courage, and both are needed when we confront the unknown.

Since the future is always unknown, it takes a certain level of courage just to get out of bed every morning. Most of us have conquered that fear so we can move on to more challenging things. Having confidence is a result of having courage. It doesn't take courage to do the things we know how to do, but it takes courage to do something new, such as starting a business of our own. It takes courage to display what we have to offer in the hope that someone will like it and want to buy it. It takes courage to face criticism from friends and strangers who don't see things the same way we do, and it takes courage to be an artist who is willing to invest our time, money, and passions into an art form and then watch how people react. The results can be highly encouraging or deeply discouraging, but you'll notice that the word *courage* is the root of both of those words.

We must have the courage to take our chances, and we're bound to get mixed reactions from people. The ones who respond positively are our potential clients, and the ones who respond negatively or not at all are not meant to be working with us, at least not at this time. Move on. Everyone has their own personal tastes, and we want to serve the ones who are in harmony with our personal vision or style.

Be aware that if we base our happiness and definition of success on how other people react, then we're not following our inner guide. Rather, we're giving more value to the opinions of others than we are to our own intuition. There's a difference between responding to feedback from the world around us and letting the world around us make our decisions for us.

Responding to feedback empowers us to make our own choices about how we want to respond. However, depending on the outside world to tell us what we should be doing is akin to surrendering our personal decisions to the opinions of others. That's very dangerous because they don't have our lessons to learn, and they don't have our gifts to give, so they don't understand the path we're on. Some will probably think we're foolish to even believe there is a path.

When we look to others to tell us what we should be doing, we are looking in the wrong direction. We are looking outside of ourselves for answers that can only be found in our hearts. When we do that, we are leaving our most precious decisions up to someone else. The key to personal fulfillment is to look inward, searching through our own imagination and feelings for the dreams and visions that excite us. We must search for the feelings that arouse our passions and then be willing to follow that path of adventure, just to see where it goes. When we do that, we will be rewarded in ways that are inconceivable to the average person.

Being able to earn a good income through the effective use of our talents is the kind of reward that will motivate most of us. We'd be happy just to earn some money while we're doing something we enjoy. However, the ultimate goal of self-discovery and personal development is to establish a sense of balance among all four of our human aspects, the physical, emotional, intellectual, and living parts of our existence. We want to live a physically healthy lifestyle that allows us to express ourselves emotionally in such a way that we can intellectually figure how to get paid while we fulfill the very reason we are alive.

Consciously or unconsciously, our real goal is to achieve balance of these essential aspects, regardless of what kind of work we do. We all want to be healthy; we all want to be emotionally understood, loved, and appreciated; and we all want to be smart enough to earn a good income while we feel as if what we do matters and we're not wasting our time.

As artists, we've chosen to pursue mastery of our lives by expressing our ideas and emotions in an artistic way. Any industry or career can offer a path to this sense of balance, but we must first decide what our purpose in life is and then use that understanding as the starting point to go on our own journey of discovery and development. The unconscious urge to achieve a sense of balance in our lives is the same for everyone, but the path we take to achieve that balance is unique to each of us.

Confidence is like a muscle, and it can only be developed with practice. It requires having the courage to do new things, the willingness to fail sometimes, and the determination to get up and start over again and again and again, as many times as we fail. Confidence and determination go hand in hand with a sense of commitment.

Commitment brings results. Without commitment, the first obstacle you meet will discourage you from going further. Commitment comes from within us, and it is directly related to the amount of desire we have for the results we want to achieve. Having a strong desire for something creates in us a sense of determination and a willingness to go for it, and we then make a commitment that we will not stop until we achieve the result we desire.

Commitment gives us a sense of determination, a do-or-die kind of feeling. It comes from that part of us that declares, "Give me liberty or give me death!" While I may or may not get everything I'm going after, I prefer to live a life of commitment to my dream as I embark on an adventurous journey that pursues something bigger than my current self. I prefer to contribute and be a participant rather than to live and die on the sidelines of life as a spectator. Perhaps it's better to regret doing some things than it is to regret not having done some of the things that were possible.

Respecting our creative spirit gives us the feeling that it's better to live a life that is adventurous and interesting than to live a long, secure, but boring life, doing something that pays the bills but doesn't satisfy the soul or the emotions. For some of us, it can be a tough decision to go after a dream, and for others it's a no-brainer. The real question is, why are we here? We may not always have a job, but we always have a purpose, and if we know what our purpose is, then our job is to fulfill our purpose. Our personal responsibility is to figure how we want to do that.

We know we have talent, and we know we enjoy using it. We think it would be nice if we could get paid for doing something we enjoy, but let's get real. Does anybody else really care? We ask ourselves, "Am I good enough? If I am, how would I start? What are the steps I need to take, and which step would I take first?"

Let me answer a few of those questions. The first step is to make a commitment to follow your heart and go in the direction of your dream. That's something only you can do. It's a great feeling to be committed to something bigger than your current level of awareness, because it causes you to go on an inner search and discovery mission, to see what you have to offer, and that in itself can be exciting. It all starts within us, and we need to look there before we look at the world around us for guidance. That *is* the secret of the artist's creativity. We know where to look. We look within.

As artists—and by that I mean any and all creative people—we have been blessed with an awareness of our inner selves that many people ignore or are totally unaware of. They say they have no imagination, but that's not true. They have just as much imagination as anyone else, but they simply don't imagine anything new with it.

As artists, we depend on the use of our imaginations to conceive of our next project. We are emotionally passionate about what we want to do and how we want to do it. We have ideas and feelings that we want to express, and these are hidden within us and invisible to the world around us until we bring them out of our imaginations and make them tangible.

It's the job of the artist to transform the ideas that can only be found in the imagination into something that can be experienced by others in the physical world. We make imaginary things tangible.

Becoming aware of our inner world is best accomplished through the practice of meditation, the act of relaxing the conscious mind and experiencing the silence of our subconscious thoughts. Through meditation, we can become aware of our innermost feelings and ideas. It offers us a way of becoming conscious of our deeper motivations, and it offers a path to finding more creative solutions to our concerns.

Now it's time for a self-assessment. For this you will need something to write on, and you will want to save your notes. We will be making a blueprint or a guidebook for ourselves, and we will start by making a list of the things we are currently able to do and that we enjoy doing at our current level of development. This is a list of the kinds of skills we currently have to offer to the world. These are things that really interest us and that we would not get bored doing, since we plan to be doing it as a career.

Start writing this list now, and carry a notepad with you to continually add ideas to the list throughout the next several days and weeks. It's important that you write them down so you can watch the list grow as you expand your self-awareness. It's not enough to know that you have skills to offer; you must see it in writing. A list or blueprint is the first step in taking an idea out of the imagination and making it into something physical.

Make another list of the things you would enjoy learning to do or that you recognize that you will need to learn in order to do the things that interest you. This may require taking specific classes or learning to use new tools. Consider things such as where you want to live and what you want to do with your talent. Define the payoff you want to receive in return for all the work you're going to be doing.

As professional artists, we are embarking on an exciting lifetime of learning and discovery. We'll never discover it all, so let's get started now so we can get the most from the time we have. It's also good to remember the old saying that "if you do what you love, you'll never work a day in your life." That phrase doesn't mean that we would love to do nothing; it means that if we enjoy what we do, our activities won't fit the negative sense that the word *work* often implies.

If we love the work we're doing, then the joy and fulfillment of the work is the greatest reward we receive, and the money we earn is a bonus. It's that kind of internal creative drive that offers us a great lifestyle in return for taking the time to develop our talents. You'll notice that creative people don't quit working just because they reach a certain age. There is no retirement age for creativity. Remember the analogy of the apple tree. If it stops producing fruit, it dies. The creative juices are what keep our minds active and healthy, and they help keep us alive as long as we keep them flowing.

Once we've made that inner commitment to earn money with our talent, it's time for a little paperwork. Print a business card. It's a simple step, but it's a huge declaration to ourselves, and it's something we can give to the world that states publicly that we are in business and we are offering our services accordingly.

Having something printed adds legitimacy to our personal vision, and seeing our business name in print somehow makes it more official. As simple as a business card may be, it's a printed document that lists our name, our product or service, and a way for people to contact us.

A business card is an inexpensive gift that we can give to people. It's always nice to give something, and a business card gives a client the feeling that we are actually located somewhere, we are serious about whatever is being offered on our card, and it becomes a seed for something that may pay off sometime in the future. A business card can be dredged out of a card file easier than a memory can be brought back from the past.

By this time, we've acknowledged that we are artists, and we've decided to earn some money with our talents, so we've gotten some business cards printed, and we've created some kind of artwork to sell. Anything is a start, and we'll always be producing more. We'll constantly be expanding our talents and improving our skills each time we produce something new. Our talents are the best thing we can invest in, because the more we use our talents, the more talented we become. No object in the physical world works that way. Physically, the more we use something, the more it wears out, but with our talents, the more we use them, the stronger they become. Nothing else offers us that kind of return on our investment.

Once we establish ourselves in a particular market, the market will tell us what they want by giving us commissions. They will ask us if we can do something specific for them. Artists thrive on commissions. Commissions are a form of positive feedback that tells us that we are on the right path with our style or subject matter. For us, accepting the commission is simply a question of whether we are willing to adapt our style to their particular needs and what dollar amount would they be willing to pay for such a service.

Each time a request or commission is offered, our personal and creative lives have the opportunity to take a new and exciting turn in the direction of the request. If it interests us, it becomes a window of opportunity. If it's not something that suits our style or if it doesn't match with our personal values, we have the freedom to decline the request because it would only be a detour from the path we are on or a distraction to the direction we want our lives to take.

Over time, our personal style and unique form of expression will naturally evolve in many ways as we develop new techniques and experiment with new tools, subjects, and materials. Creative occupations are built on a foundation of continued learning and constant discovery of new ways to express ourselves. Life's learning is an endless journey, and that's what keeps it interesting.

Chapter 7

THE CREATIVE POWER OF THOUGHTS AND BELIEFS

All creative expression begins with a thought. We get an idea, a feeling that we want to say something or make something. Perhaps our curiosity is sparked in some way, and it urges us to experiment and discover what happens when we mix different things together. We make plans for the future or we sketch out a design for something we might build. These are all examples of thoughts, and they have the power to change our lives because they motivate us to take action.

Thoughts are the most powerful things in our lives. Our thoughts work like a compass that guides the direction our lives go in. Our thoughts determine our attitudes and how we feel about something, and our attitudes determine how we behave toward that thing or situation. We are expressing our thoughts when we create a work of art.

As artists, when we are working on a project, we are literally expressing our feelings based on what we think about the subject we're working on, as well as such factors as how we feel about the client who commissioned the artwork. It's apparent that we do better work for someone we love than we tend to do for someone we resent or wish we didn't have to work for. It's important to appreciate and respect our clients, because the quality of the relationship will be reflected in the quality of the work we do. Our thoughts affect how we feel and consequently how we behave toward everything, including ourselves.

Success in life flows from our "beingness," which is the sum of all that we are, including our attitudes, actions, appearance, behavior, etc., all rolled up into our unique personality. Let me explain.

Our deepest beliefs show up in our everyday actions and attitudes, and they affect everything that we are and everything that we do. Everything we've learned and experienced up to this point has made us into who, what, and how we are being at this moment. Most people believe that success flows in the direction of "have-be-do." That is to say that if I *have* a million dollars, then I would *be* a millionaire, and I could *do* the things millionaires do. But that's not the way life works. That's putting the results ahead of the activity.

The way life works is "be-do-have." That is to say that if I will *be* the person I want to be, then I will *do* the things that kind of person would do, and I will *have* the results that those actions create. Having the results we want starts with being the person we were meant to be. In the beginning, other people may not see us as being the person we believe we are, but that's not a problem, because we will evolve into being that person the more we live with the belief and knowledge that *we already are that person.*

It may be helpful and encouraging to think of ourselves once again in terms of the apple tree. Every fruitful tree starts out as a seed that doesn't bear any physical resemblance to the tree it will eventually grow up to be. In that seed are all the essential elements the plant needs in order to grow into a beautifully blossoming and fruitful tree. With a little nourishment and a supportive environment, the seed will go through all the steps it needs to take to fulfill its destiny and eventually be the tree it was always meant to be.

All the potential for everything we are meant to be is in the original seed or idea. We just have to go through the process of letting each step naturally unfold along the way.

What we are now may not bear any resemblance to what we believe we are capable of becoming, but if we sense that we are meant to be that great producer of creative fruit that is represented by the mature apple tree, then we will accept each step along the way. Every step is an exciting phase in the never-ending journey we go on when we discover and develop our unlimited personal potential.

Everything we do begins with an idea of who we think we are. This is our self-image. We always live up to (or down to) the internal image we hold of ourselves, and herein lies the key to having whatever we want. We always behave in accordance with whatever we believe to be true about ourselves, and as a result of our behavior, we create certain results in our lives. These results usually reinforce what we already believe, since our beliefs tend to focus our attention on things we recognize, and we simply don't notice the things we're not tuned into. Since our beliefs focus our attention on specific things, our lives often become an expanding cycle of repeated experiences, unless we intentionally take on some new challenges and are willing to think outside the box.

The key to being the person we want to be and achieving the results we want to have is to know that we already are that person. We just have to live up to the standards of that person and not let outside forces detour us from our path. As artists, we realize that our imagination is just as real as the physical world that surrounds us. The events we experience in our imagination have just as much power to influence us and alter our lives as any outer events we might experience. We believe in the things we imagine, but other people can't participate in our imaginary events because our dreams and visions aren't in a form that can be shared or experienced by others.

That becomes the job and the challenge that faces every artist: to transform what is imagined or felt only by us into something that others can experience. This challenge applies to each project we take on, and it applies to the total life we create for ourselves as we go through each step along our journey.

We are already behaving in exact accordance with who we believe ourselves to be at this moment. We've created the current situations we find ourselves in as a result of being who we have been up to this point. If we like the situations we are in, then we must keep doing the things that are working for us. However, if there's a need for a change in any area of our lives, this is the key to making that change: we must see ourselves in our imagination as the person we want to be, already having the kind of business clients we enjoy working with and receiving the kind of compensation and living the lifestyle we want and are proud of.

We act in accordance with our beliefs, so it's important that we recognize and believe in the power of the images we hold in front of us when we meditate or dream. The clearer and more vivid the image is and the more we can make that image feel real to us, the more power and impact that image will have on our behavior and the actions we take.

Through meditation or relaxed visualization exercises, we can immerse ourselves in that image and enjoy the feelings we get when we spend time with our imagination. This is not just freestyle dreaming, but rather, it is a relaxed and focused visualization activity with our life as the theme of the exercise. This is perhaps the most important part of the creative process, where we merge our vision with our feelings, and we make them both believable to our subconscious mind. Once that deeper part of us accepts and believes in the reality of our vision, whatever it may be, that seed will have taken root, and the process of unfoldment will begin.

Once we've imagined the person we want to be, if we don't already believe that we are that person, we need to spend more time meditating on the images we associate with our desires and focus our attention on the feelings the new images give us. Feelings or emotions are an essential part of our creative process, and learning how to control them is as important as learning how to use a paintbrush or any other physical tool. Developing a clear mental image of ourselves and packing that image with such positive emotions as intense desire, enthusiasm, and the joyous feeling of fulfillment helps to develop a positive belief about the reality of our vision and increases our desire for the pleasurable results. Desire + belief = having.

Having what we want requires both elements, desire and belief. If there is no desire, there will be no motivation to act and hence, no results. If there is no belief in the possibility, there will be no commitment to the effort or actions that will be required to achieve the desired results. It takes both, the desire to have or to be something and the belief that it's possible to achieve it. Those two elements will drive the creative spirit to search for and develop every step it takes to get the results we imagine.

As you believe, so shall it be. Our beliefs are powerful because it's our beliefs that make our experiences possible. That may be because we are only aware of the things that we already believe are true and we unconsciously ignore the things we don't understand. We tend to focus our attention on those things that validate what we already know and believe.

It's important to spend time every day consciously imagining ourselves accomplishing our next step in the never-ending unfoldment of our lives. Once we reach the point in our minds that we know we are artists, we will act like artists and do the things artists do. We'll express ourselves creatively, and we'll put our time and our passions into some kind of activity that will create something from whatever thoughts we come up with. Our thoughts will be converted into actions that will produce a result that we refer to as a work of art. That's just what artists do.

Actually, that's what everyone does, but the difference between the artist and the nonartistic person is that the artist is constantly creating new thought patterns and ideas, while the average person, who is just as creative, continually imagines and creates the same patterns over and over every day, so there is very little change in their daily lives. Then they say they have no imagination. The truth is, they simply have no variation in the things they imagine.

Once we have established the belief and knowledge that we are artists and that we have a valid role to play in our community, it's time to expand our self-image to include the idea that we are business people as well. If we are going to earn money with our talents, then we must realize that we are in the business of selling our artwork or our creative services. Our creative offerings can include consulting services such as interior decorators and designers or arranging professional displays for storefronts and sales conventions. We can offer any kind of service that we know anything about. The key to success in any field of endeavor is to find a need that someone has and fill it. We will be paid in accordance with the value they place on the services we offer.

As artists, we are in the business of providing a creative solution to someone's need, and our opportunities to earn money are as unlimited as our willingness to be of service.

It's time to recognize ourselves as creative business people. While each person can specialize in his or her favorite type of expression, whether it be painting or sculpture, music, poetry, illustration, jewelry, tattoos, clothing design, cheap decorative trinkets, or high-end art that sells in a New York gallery, there is a market that we can satisfy by recognizing the wants and needs of others. When it comes to earning money, it doesn't matter what form the artwork takes, as long as it serves some purpose in someone else's life and they would be willing to pay for it.

That leads us to marketing. Marketing is also related to our beingness. What kind of an artist are we being? There is money available at every level of artwork, from cute little items you might sell at a flea market to multimillion-dollar sales that happen at international art auctions.

A happy and successful life allows us to be ourselves, wherever we are at this time in our lives, and the trick is to bloom where we're planted and keep growing from there. Remember that we get paid for providing a service of some kind, so it starts by asking ourselves, "How do I enjoy expressing myself?" and then asking, "Who would benefit most from the way I express myself?" Define your market. It will probably be a reflection of you. We are most likely to attract people who are similar to us. They have similar tastes, and they like our style. It's that "birds of a feather" kind of thing. We feel most comfortable providing services to people who are most like ourselves because we understand each other.

I have met many young artists who enjoy drawing comics and cartoons. Doing the exaggerations of the character's features and creating outlandish costumes with intense colors has an appeal to some artists. So, how can this kind of artwork be used to earn money? Perhaps it would make great tattoos, or it might be an impressive image on a T-shirt. Commercial applications of recognizable characters are worth millions in the corporate world. Think of the GEICO gecko or Ronald McDonald and the related characters used for this type of corporate identity. Someone got paid to create those characters. The concept and the designs are a valuable form of art, and someone had to create them.

By printing an interesting character or design onto a T-shirt and adding a one- or two-word graphic statement, we are creatively expressing our feelings, and at the same time, we are offering the purchaser a way to share our creative sentiment in public. The more universal our statement is, the bigger the market will be for our product. By producing artwork like that, we provide a way for people to express their feelings that are similar to ours. It's a win-win situation, in that we've served our market simply by being ourselves and the amount of money we can earn will be determined by how well we market our art once we've created it.

Another way to sell comic art is to expand the artwork into

the theatrical drama of the character's personalities. When we do that, we expand our creative expressions by becoming playwrights. Now we're seeing and contributing to a bigger vision, and we're expressing our view of life through the personal interactions of our comic book characters.

Having the ability to draw things is not enough to cause people to give us money, but it's a starting point. It's not just the artwork that sells; it's what can be done with it that adds value and makes it useful to the marketplace. When something is useful to someone, they become willing and eager to pay for it.

We attract to ourselves that which we are. If we are sophisticated in our expression, we will be inclined to attract a sophisticated audience. If we're more inclined toward street art, we will attract people who relate to that type of subject matter. Regardless of what we create, people are willing to pay a price for the things that they appreciate and value.

Having started my career in a high school rock band, I remember splitting $35 a night with three other band members and thinking we were professional rock stars on our way up the ladder. It's amazing how a little financial encouragement can go a long way when you're young and full of ambition. Dreams are still wide open, and we believe that all things are possible.

Dreams do come true, but for a dream to come true, we have to have a dream to begin with. Dreams do not demand anything from us. Rather, they give something to us. They become the driving force by which we eagerly plan our time. We get excited about our dreams, and we can't wait to get back to the project we're working on. The dream inspires us to *want* to work, not *have* to work. Dreams make a big difference in our motivation. The rewards of making progress toward the things we dream about has its own motivating forces, and a little positive reinforcement moves things along faster and faster as we continue to make progress in our life's work.

I value the ability to be the one who is in control of my life. I like to set my own schedule, pick and choose my projects, and determine my own prices. I decide what my time is worth, and if my client is willing to pay the price I'm asking, then we go ahead with the project.

Personally, I love paint. I prefer pigments over pixels. I enjoy the process of spraying, brushing, and sponging the various colors together to get the results I'm looking for. The subject matter might be what the client requests, but the process of producing it is where I find my pleasure. I like to say, "You can tell me what you want, but you can't tell me how to give it to you." That's my job. For me, that *is* the art. I'm not pursuing the end results as much as I'm enjoying the process of creating it. For me, it's the journey more than the destination. The goal or destination is just an excuse to go through the enjoyable process of creating things.

Like the apple tree, I have no use for my products once I create them. With my murals, I leave them behind like the apple tree drops its fruit on the ground and doesn't care what happens to it once it lets go of it. The productive artist, like the productive fruit tree, simply moves on to create something else. To be productive is to be alive. To stop producing is to stop the flow and let things dry up and wither away.

There are ways to earn money in any area or with any style, as long as it serves the needs of others. As an artist, what business do you want to be in, or what area do you enjoy specializing in? Jewelry? Illustrations for children's books? Graphics for commercial applications? Gallery art? Tattoos? Sculpture?

Portraiture? Photography? Music? Lighting? Costume design? There is no end the list of possibilities.

My first career was as an entertainer in high school and college, and that ruined me for any kind of normal day job once I learned that I could get paid for having fun. When I outgrew my first career as a barroom entertainer, I began my career as an artist by channeling my creative urges into commercial advertising artwork for the print industry. I then got into painting signs until the computer and the vinyl letters took over in that industry. From there I airbrushed T-shirts at car shows and started doing custom artwork on cars and motorcycles. Today I enjoy painting murals for schools and on residential backyard walls.

When I paint my wall murals, I think of myself as being in the home improvement business. My artwork serves a purpose of making someone's environment more attractive or pleasant for them. I am on a mission to make this world a more beautiful place for people to live and work in. I'll never run out of work to do.

I recommend that you elevate your search for work to being on a mission where you use your unique talents to leave your mark in some way in someone else's life. Increasing the value of your job from simply being a way to earn a paycheck into being a mission to make a positive difference in the world will affect your art in a way that will be felt on an emotional level by the people who experience it. The quality of your work and the pleasure you receive from doing it will be affected by the amount of joy and passion you are willing to put into it.

Chapter 8

THE ART OF CREATING THE LIFE WE WANT

Creating what we want depends on knowing what we want. That applies to creating the plans for our next project or laying out an entire road map for our lives.

As artists, we are blessed with an abundance of imaginative ideas and passionate feelings about what we want to express and what we want to see happen in the physical world. Some of our ideas may seem bizarre and impractical, but for the artist, it's fun to imagine such things. While many things are only impractical to those who won't allow themselves to think outside of their established patterns, the artist is able to enjoy the world of the imagination just as much as the world that surrounds us.

We literally spend our lives traveling between two very real and very different dimensions, the world of the imagination that we experience when we close our eyes and dream or meditate and the physical world that we see with our eyes open and we experience with our bodies as if it were something that happens from outside of us.

The reality is that we experience both in our mind, one as a self-generated mental experience, the other as an externally generated experience that relies on our five physical senses. We make a mental interpretation of a physical sensation as being painful or pleasurable, and as we react accordingly, the experience becomes part of our permanent mental memory.

Our entire life is a mental experience that we continually add to as we grow and learn new things. The mind doesn't forget anything; it just tucks things away that we choose not to remember, and it keeps playing other things over and over that we can't forget. All of our collected memories become part of our inventory of material that we draw from when we express ourselves. The more we understand the things that are motivating us, the more we can cash in on what's working and deal appropriately with the troubling spots. Let's start by looking at some common similarities about people in general.

Something that everybody wants in life is a sense of empowerment, that feeling of having control and being able to go after and successfully achieve the things we want. It requires a belief that dreams do come true, and they do, but in order for a dream to come true, we have to have a dream. That leads to the question of what is it that you personally want? Define it. Describe it and imagine it in detail. If it's a particular project, imagine the finished result in its perfect completed form. Become excited about it, and then use your intellectual ability to work backward from your completed vision and figure out or imagine the steps you have to take along the way to get to that perfect end result.

As we imagine each step along the way, our imagination will cause our physical actions to go in the direction of our vision. Everything starts with the imagination, and then by adding the belief that it's possible, our emotions become aroused with desire. As we become enthusiastic about the intended results, our lives begin to move in the direction of our vision. Our vision, plus belief, inspires action, which leads to results. This process is the same whether we are creating a specific project or an entire life.

If our imagination is about creating an entire lifestyle, then we must visualize ourselves in the situations we associate with our definition of success. We see ourselves living that lifestyle in our preferred location, being surrounded by the people we serve or work with, and we see ourselves getting the reaction we want, financially, socially, and emotionally, from the kind of work we are doing. Be excited about that imaginary experience! With the positive emotional feeling and the belief that it's already real, even though it's still in its imaginary state, the creative process begins to proceed according to our belief. This process works with the smallest projects as well as with our entire lives.

The mind creates whatever it believes to be real. As you believe, so shall it be. The subconscious mind cannot tell the difference between what is real and what is imagined. Both experiences are interpreted by the subconscious as having happened, and either type of experience has the power to change the course of our actions and thereby affect the outcome of our lives. We must treasure our dreams and visions and have respect for our creative abilities. The power of our imagination blended with the power of belief holds the keys to having everything we want.

Desire is a feeling of hunger or lack, and while it may be an unpleasant feeling in itself, it can be a positive driving force in motivating us to take action. Without a desire for something new or without a sense of dissatisfaction with the current situation we find ourselves in, there is no motivating force to support the forward movement for us personally or for society as a whole.

Getting what we want depends on knowing what we want, and there is a way to have it. Keeping in mind that all people want some basic things, if we can offer some of those things to our market, the market will come to us as their source, and we can receive the things we want in return. Other people have the things that we want, and getting those things for ourselves is simply a matter of exchanging what we have to offer for the equivalent value of the things that they have to offer. It's the basic act of bartering our products and services for their products and services, using money as a convenient form of exchange for whatever values we establish.

We're participating in basic marketplace economics when we provide a creative solution to the needs of the people in exchange for their money. This law of trading our time and talent in exchange for getting the things we want applies to our lives, whether we are working at a conventional nine-to-five job for a consistent paycheck or if we are doing separate projects, each for a variable price.

Let's start with some basic truths about human beings in general. We all want to be loved. We all want to be respected. We all want to be cared for or cared about by someone. We want to feel like we matter, and we want to feel like we can make a difference in our world. That leads us to some serious consideration about our career and our lives as artists.

How do we incorporate these basic truths into the work that we do, regardless of the form our artwork takes? Common sense tells us that we can only give what we have, and we can't give what we don't have. In order to create a masterpiece, the artist must be a master, so the quality of our work will depend on the quality of the artist as a person.

From the perspective of the imagination, the artist is a tool that it uses to channel its unlimited ideas from the dimension of imagination into the dimension of physical reality. As artists, the steps we go through in order to produce our artwork are the actual steps of transforming the imagination into physical reality. We are the link between what is in the imagination and what becomes tangible or real in the dimension of the physical world. What we experience in our personal imaginations must be transformed into something physical so that it can be experienced and shared with others. That is the challenge that faces every artist.

We have control over the skills we want to develop, and we have the freedom to choose our subject matter and tools, as well as the methods and materials we prefer to work with. Having the ability to imagine something different than what is currently happening in our lives gives us the power to change things by the effective use of our imaginations and our beliefs.

There is a way to have the things we want in life, and it requires striking a balance between the four aspects of our lives: the physical, the intellectual, the emotional, and the power of being alive. Another way to say it is that we need to balance our need for financial success with our need to express ourselves emotionally while maintaining healthy physical habits and all the while feeling like we're fulfilling our purpose for being alive.

I refer to this method of getting what we want as "the shopping list." A shopping list is more than a wish list. Wishes are things that would be nice to have but for the most part we aren't eager or willing to pay for. A shopping list, on the other hand, is a list of things we actually intend to go after, and when we put things on a shopping list, we actually expect to pay for them when we go out to get them.

Here's how the shopping list works.
- Take four separate pieces of paper, and at the top of one sheet, write the words: "My Perfect (whatever you want) Physically."
- On the second sheet of paper, write the words: "My Perfect (whatever) Emotionally."
- On the third sheet, write the words: "My Perfect (whatever) Intellectually."
- On the fourth sheet of paper, write the words: "My Perfect (whatever) Spiritually."

This shopping list exercise can be applied to anything we want to have in life, from our perfect home or automobile to the perfect partner or the perfect career. The reason this shopping list works is because it works on us. It causes us to focus our attention on our highest ambitions and desires while forcing us to balance the four elements that make us human. The list won't change the world around us, but it will have an effect on us by raising our vibrations to the level where we will be in harmony with the things we desire, rather than feeling separated from the things we want.

For our example, let's look at how we can create the perfect career for ourselves. I'm going to use examples from my own life, so your list will have some very different things listed.

Page one would look something like this:

My Perfect Career Physically:
- Is located in my home
- Has a large, well-lit studio with an inspiring view
- Is within driving distance of art galleries and creative communities
- Is located in a warm climate (be specific about the city if it's important)
- Allows me to work outdoors
- Offers me opportunities to travel to interesting places

Continue to fill the first sheet in with physical characteristics. Take a note pad with you wherever you go, and write down things throughout the day as you think of them. Add things to the list for at least a couple of weeks. You'll think of new considerations at the most unexpected times, so keep your notebook handy.

Page two might look like this:

My Perfect Career Emotionally:
- Keeps me enthusiastic about the work I do
- Gets me excited about the people I meet and the places I get to visit
- Allows me to express my love for beautiful things
- Gives me respect in my community
- Is a way for me to express the joy I find in my favorite subjects
- Gives me pleasure when I see the faces of my satisfied customers
- Allows me to express my opinions

Continue to imagine the emotional qualities of your perfect career and how it makes you feel when you are actively living it daily. Add these positive feelings and the things that trigger them to your list over the next few days and weeks.

Page three might look like this:

My Perfect Career Intellectually:
- Challenges me to keep learning new things
- Allows me to set my own prices
- Provides the income I desire
- Allows me to set my own schedule
- Surrounds me with other creative people
- Gives me the free time I desire
- Allows me to experiment with new materials and technologies

Keep adding things to your list for several days and weeks as you refine your dreams and visions. This list is becoming the blueprint for your life.

Page four might look like this:

My Perfect Career Spiritually:
- Just feels like this is what I'm supposed to be doing
- Allows me to affect people in a positive and meaningful way
- Makes my work feel like more of a mission than just a job
- Is more important to me than the money I earn
- Satisfies me in ways words can't express

As we think about the qualities we want our perfect career to include, we need to write them down and keep adding them to our list. It doesn't really matter what category a certain desire would fall into, because they all interact with each other. The important thing is that they get on the list somewhere, so we can see all the pieces of the puzzle as we start to put the whole picture together.

Here's how the list becomes effective. Everything we wrote on the list is either a quality we already possess or one we want to develop in our inventory of good personal qualities. As we acknowledge and congratulate ourselves on having the good qualities that are working for us, we can also see the areas where things are lacking, and this is where we need to work on ourselves to develop those things necessary to feel completely satisfied in that area.

While we continually work on ourselves to strengthen and polish the good qualities that are working for us, we also need to develop the new qualities we are currently lacking. What we are doing is adjusting our personal vibrations to be more in tune with the higher vibrations or vision of our perfect career.

This exercise works because we are working on ourselves. We can't change other people, and we have limited ability to change the entire world, but we can change ourselves through our thinking, and we need to be the change we want to experience. We are not trying to change the world into something that works better for us. Rather, we are changing the only thing we have control over, our "self" and our personal view of things.

We are constantly changing ourselves into the person we want to be by expanding our awareness and our intellectual understanding in such a way that it continually makes us grow into a different person as we become our own work of art. The master becomes the masterpiece.

Chapter 9

THERE IS NO COMPETITION TO BEING YOURSELF

When we look outside of ourselves and we see other people doing the kinds of things we would like to be doing, some of us will see those people as competition or challengers for the rewards available in the marketplace. Others will see those who have accomplished the kinds of things that we would like to accomplish as being mentors or role models to learn from. If they can do it, then we can do it; we just have to figure out what they did.

The rewards for living a successful life aren't always measured by results in the marketplace. The greatest rewards for a life well lived are found in the heart, in the way we feel every day as we go about the business of living. Are we on the right path? I don't know that there is right or wrong path, so the important question is, "Am I on *my* path?"

Some advice says it's best to follow the road map that's been laid out by others, while others tell us to make our own path and leave a map for someone else to follow. I'm not sure if it makes a difference as to which approach works best, as long as we get where we want to end up. So again, let's define our destination.

My attitude about having a goal or a destination is that a destination is really only a good excuse to go on a journey. Yes, I want to achieve the end result that I define as my goal, but I also want to enjoy the process of achieving that goal. I have to enjoy the journey. I have to feel good about how I go about getting the things I want. My goal as well as the methods I choose to achieve my goals have to be in alignment with my values, my ethics, and my sense of fair play for me to feel that I actually deserve to have achieved the results. I don't want to short circuit the system as an attempt to get something for nothing. The self-esteem and self-confidence that is developed by paying the price for something is in itself a personal reward that I carry with me wherever I go.

Confidence shows in our eyes and in our actions. It shows in the way we walk into a room. It becomes a big part of the way the public perceives us, as well as having its effect on our own self-esteem. The confidence that we get from knowing that we paid the price for what we've accomplished is as great a reward as any form of financial return.

Think about the Olympic athlete who runs several miles every day in preparation for the challenge of participating in the big event. The goal is not only to be in the Olympics, but to win the gold medal once you get there. What if they don't make the cut? What if they gave it their best and committed every spare minute and dime to the dream, and they just weren't good enough to get into the Olympics? So what? Look at how much further they traveled down the road of adventure than they would have if they didn't have a goal in the first place.

A goal is just an excuse to take our lives in a direction that excites us.

It's the journey that gets us to the destination, so we must enjoy the journey. We're going to be on one for the rest of our lives. Having a destination points us in the direction we want our lives to go in, and it sets up the path we want to take to get there. Having a big dream brings out the best in us.

We all have the potential to do great things, but we often lack the motivation. Complacency and being easily satisfied with average things in life does not require the passion and drive that a sense of great accomplishment requires. However, a sense of having accomplished something great is a personal issue, not a universal concept.

I have watched Special Olympics events where young kids with very real challenges are accomplishing greatness in their lives. While those accomplishments won't make the headlines in the daily news, they do change the lives of the participants, as well as the spectators who witness the struggles and determination of the athletes. Greatness can be found on many levels. Greatness is determined more by the size of the challenge we are willing to take on than it is by the end result we achieve.

So, I'll ask you on a very personal level, what is your greatest challenge? What is it that you would like to accomplish during your time on earth? Write it down. Determine what things bring you pleasure and satisfy your sense of inner peace and prosperity. Define what you can offer to the world, and imagine the effect your work can have on your community. What do you enjoy doing? What are you good at? What would you like to learn or get better at?

These are personal questions that only you can answer, and

the answers only matter to you. No one else needs to know the answers, but if you work with the responses you come up with, you will be setting yourself on a path that will be financially, emotionally, and spiritually rewarding to you, as well as to the people you choose to serve.

There is no competition for the things you want. No one is competing to learn your lessons, and no one else has your gifts to give. Each of us has our own reasons for being here, and we each have our own way of looking at things, as well as our own unique way of expressing ourselves. There is no competition to being yourself. Who else can you be? You can copy people, and you can imitate others, but you can never *be* anybody but you. In that, you're stuck, so you might as well make the most of it and be yourself all the way!

By creating things and offering services the world is willing to pay for, you can write your own script and draw your own map. Your talents are your greatest assets, and your unique gifts become your ticket to go on the journey of a lifetime.

The Summary

A FEW THINGS TO CONSIDER

No one gets paid just because they have talent. We get paid because we provide a service with our talent. If the service we provide involves one or more of our talents, we will probably enjoy the work we do, and we will do good work because we are enjoying ourselves. We will probably earn good money because we are doing good work. But again, we are not being paid just because we have talent; we are being paid because we are *providing something of value* with our talents. That is the key to earning money. It's not enough just to have the potential; it must be developed into a form that can be shared and experienced by others and then marketed in a way that the public can find it and buy it.

While the conventional job market for artists may be slim, the opportunity to be of service is unlimited, and with each opportunity to serve comes the opportunity to get paid. In our society, a person gets paid in proportion to the service he or she renders to others. If we want to increase our wealth, we must find ways to increase the value of our service. That can be done through more effective marketing so we can reach more people, as well as by improving the quality of our work. The more we do something, the better we should get at doing it. Improved speed and better quality go hand in hand with experience. Our minds keep finding ways to streamline things.

We all have a purpose for being here. We each have certain unique gifts to offer, and we each have our individual lessons to learn. If we use our gifts, we will learn many lessons, and life will be meaningful and filled with fascinating adventures. We will engage ourselves in activities that are interesting and in harmony with our personal goals and aspirations. The work we do will be a blessing to our communities, and we will live productive and fulfilling lives.

If we don't make use of our unique gifts and talents, we will never know our true selves, that inner power of the imagination that is expressing itself through us. That power is the power of life, beating our hearts and breathing our lungs, unconsciously doing all that operational stuff for us while we get to make the personal decisions about what we want to do with our time every day. As artists, we get to creatively express our free will as long as we have that power expressing itself through us.

Running an art business is no different in principle than running any other kind of service for the public. Every business provides a service to its customers, and that service requires the business owner to have some specific skills and abilities in order to understand the customer's needs and how best to address situations. The success of any business is dependent on being able to imagine the best solutions and take the most appropriate actions to efficiently meet the needs of the client. The business of art just happens to be based on providing imaginative and creative solutions to the needs and wants of that segment of the public that appreciates art, whether it's in the form of advertising art, T-shirt designs, jewelry, tattoos, fine arts, decorative items, sculptures, gift items, and so on. When it comes to earning money, the type of art we produce doesn't matter as much as the purpose it serves in the marketplace.

Whatever we choose to do, it all starts with the same challenge that faces every artist: to take an idea from the realm of the imagination and transform it into something that can be experienced in the realm of the physical world. That is our job and our challenge.

No sense of accomplishment comes without overcoming some challenging obstacles. Imagination is needed to see the possibilities, and courage is needed to begin something new. With courage comes the confidence to keep going and growing. Reputations are built over time. Fame can be purchased with enough advertising dollars, but a reputation lives on after the fame dies away. I encourage the development of the reputation first, based on solid business principles of providing great service, and let the fame develop on its own.

As artists, we create the future by bringing some of the unlimited possibilities out of the imagination and transforming them into something that becomes a part of the physical world. That's quite an accomplishment, and it's something to be proud of! The mind speaks in pictures. It understands and responds emotionally to images it sees or imagines. The visual image has power, and as we get better at working with the effect that the image can have on people, as artists we have tremendous influence on the public's perception of whatever subject matter we turn our attention to. As with any power, it can be used for good or evil, and the decision is in the hands of those who know how to use it.

We may not always have a job, but we always have a purpose, and if we understand what our purpose is, then our job is to fulfill that purpose.

Best wishes always,
Jim Gardner

About the Author

Jim Gardner earned a bachelor's degree in art from the University of Wisconsin in 1973. Having worked his way through college as an entertainer, he worked in the music business for several years before falling back on his college art training. He began working at ad agencies and print shops, painting signs on the side and airbrushing T-shirts at car shows. This evolved into custom painting cars and motorcycles and today he paints wall murals around the Phoenix metropolitan area. He is also the author of *Artists Are Like Apple Trees: A Guidebook for Success in Music, Art and Theatre.* He lives in Mesa, Arizona, with his wife and 2 dogs.

For more information visit www.MuralsByGardner.com.

Printed in the United States
By Bookmasters